Ideology After Poststructuralism

Social Sciences Research Centre Series
Interpreting the Modern World

Editors: Ricca Edmondson and Mark Haugaard
National University of Ireland, Galway

Many key problems now facing humankind demand multidisciplinary analysis, but at the same time academic specialisation is on the increase. Hence this series encourages original research which challenges conventional disciplinary divisions. This interdisciplinary approach is not merely a matter of combining existing views that have been kept apart by arbitrary institutionalised divisions. More significantly, it also aims at reshaping existing research paradigms through a process of open dialogue.

Ideology After Poststructuralism

Edited by
Siniša Malešević and Iain MacKenzie

Pluto Press
LONDON • STERLING, VIRGINIA

in association with SSRC

First published 2002 by Pluto Press
345 Archway Road, London N6 5AA
and 22883 Quicksilver Drive,
Sterling, VA 20166–2012, USA

www.plutobooks.com

British Library Cataloguing in Publication Data
A catalogue record for this book is available from the British Library

ISBN 0 7453 1807 X hardback

Library of Congress Cataloging in Publication Data
Ideology after poststructuralism / edited by Siniša Malešević and Iain
MacKenzie.
       p. cm.
   ISBN 0–7453–1807–X
   1. Ideology. 2. Poststructuralism. I. Malešević, Siniša. II. MacKenzie,
Iain M.
   HM 641 .I32 2002
   140—dc21

                                                            2001004547

10   9   8   7   6   5   4   3   2   1

Designed and produced for Pluto Press by
Chase Publishing Services, Fortescue, Sidmouth EX10 9QG
Typeset from disk by Stanford DTP Services, Towcester
Printed in the European Union by TJ International, Padstow, England

Contents

Acknowledgement

We would like to thank the British Academy, the School of Politics at Queen's University Belfast and the Social Science Research Centre, National University of Ireland, Galway for their generous support of the conference 'Ideology After Poststructuralism' which gave rise to the papers included in this volume.

For Luka, Kathryn and Sam

Introduction
de Tracy's Legacy

Iain MacKenzie and Siniša Malešević

Unlike many other concepts in social and political theory, ideology is not an illegitimate child. We know that its father was Count Antoine Louis Claude Destutt de Tracy and that the date of its birth was 1796. We also know that de Tracy had grand designs for his firstborn – to become a universal and integral science of all ideas. More than anything else the father of ideology wanted his offspring to transcend and surpass the ideas that had motivated the French Revolution and gained dominance in its immediate aftermath. For de Tracy the aim of ideology was 'to give a complete knowledge of our intellectual faculties, and to deduce from that knowledge the first principles of all other branches of our knowledge' (de Tracy, 1826–27). In other words, the father of ideology shared the ultimate goal of the Enlightenment movement – to establish a solid and unquestionable method by which correct ideas could be scientific-ally identified so as to foster the use of reason in the governance of human affairs for the betterment of society as a whole. This grand science of ideas was thus conceived as the final, ultimate and only measure of human intellectual capacity.

We also know that de Tracy was an overambitious father. With the benefit of hindsight it is all too clear that de Tracy's brainchild failed to live up to his expectations and the science of ideology was not to be. On the contrary, in a parodic and tragicomic historical twist, the concept invented by de Tracy has acquired rather different meanings, most of which are associated in one way or another with systematically or intentionally distorted truths. Ever since Napoleon's denunciation of 'the ideologues', the term ideology has been deployed with derogatory connotations, typically to discredit an opponent's views, actions or intentions as no more than a set of sophisticated lies. In this most stark example of the dialectical turn of Enlightenment aspirations, the dream of a science of ideas has become the nightmare of blinkered obscurantism. It would seem that de Tracy, if only he could know, would have to admit that whatever

1

hopes one has for one's children the fact remains that they carve out their own lives in directions wholly unforeseen by their parents.

This admission often leaves parents with a sense of failure. Such feelings are best overcome, though, by realising that one's legacy is often expressed at deeper, more fundamental levels than one first assumes. This is certainly the case with de Tracy. Firstly, it is often overlooked that de Tracy bequeathed much more to intellectual life than the naming of a single term. His concept marks a significant contribution to two hundred years (and counting) of discussion on the possibility of using analytic, systematically gathered and organised knowledge of human values and ideas to advance society. Although his aim of building the all-embracing genealogy of human knowledge that would provide us with a master key to the human spirit was a failure, the overall tenor of his project remains central to social and political investigation. De Tracy's primary goal was to overcome the hegemony of religious and metaphysical explanations of ideas in order to identify a method for critical investigation of the sources and development of knowledge. By asking the right questions he should undoubtedly be considered as a key figure in the development of modern sociology and philosophy of knowledge. Secondly, de Tracy's ambition to find the simple, practical and reliable tools for theoretically grounded and informed political action has led generations of others to recognise the necessity of developing coherent, systematic and realistic social and political world-views, today known as ideologies – liberalism, socialism, conservatism, feminism, etc. – thus attempting to integrate social and political theory with the practical politics of everyday life. Here too, the outcome of actions that de Tracy has triggered matter much more than his own modest results. Thirdly, de Tracy was among the first who anticipated the necessary link between knowledge, modernity and domination. Long before it was applauded by Comte, reluctantly accepted by Weber and denounced by Foucault, de Tracy had come to understand the central role that the new breed of intellectuals, the new priests of modernity, had in the construction of truth. While de Tracy, in keeping with his Enlightenment surroundings, saw these new intellectuals as the vanguard of social and political progress, we should not let his elitism and intellectual authoritarianism cloud our view of the legacy he left behind. What is important is his implicit acknowledgement of the deep link between power and knowledge in modernity.

Despite the fact that de Tracy's vision of a unified science of ideas is itself an idea generally consigned to history, his conception of ideology – with all that it implies about the relationship between theory and practice, the role of intellectuals and the status of knowledge in the modern world – has become a site of deep contestation and the springboard for many of what we take to be the most innovative and challenging ideas of contemporary social and political theory. The surest evidence of this is the fact that there are very few major social and political theorists who did not develop in one form or another even a rudimentary theory of ideology. Of course, one must be careful of assigning too great a role to de Tracy because our contemporary concerns with ideology typically stem from a lineage that takes as its starting point the work of Marx and Engels. In Marx and Engels, we have both an account of the generation of ideas and an account of the conditions that would have to be met for those ideas to merit the claim that they are fully adequate to the world around us. In short, ideology was historicised by Marx and Engels. Their account of the different ideas that dominate different economic systems in different historical epochs gave renewed impetus to the idea that the study of ideology was a core component of any serious social and political philosophy. Perhaps more importantly, Marx and Engels bequeathed to the study of ideology the idea that under conditions of post-capitalist economic production, when production is no longer riven with class division, there will be no dominant ideologies to bolster false claims as to the nature of social and political reality. This claim has generated a vast array of speculation on the possibility of non-ideological social and political interaction, and it would not be an exaggeration to say that much of the most innovative work on ideology has been that which has faced head-on the twin demands of an historicised and, in some respects, all-embracing sense of ideology and an account of the disappearance, now or in the future, of ideologically tainted forms of social and political life.

We can see this if we look at the range of discussions on ideology after Marx and Engels. To name a few, this concern is central to the work of Lenin, Bernstein, Gramsci, Althusser, Geertz, Mannheim, Marcuse, Habermas, Gouldner, Parsons, Boudon, Freeden and Žižek. Of course, these theoretical approaches to ideology differ in many ways. Some have focused on the origins of ideology, locating it in the capitalist mode of production (such as the structural Marxists), others were concerned with its psychological powers, seeing ideology as a fantasy of enjoyment (the cultural psychoanalysts, for example), some have concentrated on ideologies as cultural systems (as with the symbolic anthropologists), others have emphasised its societal function, perceiving it as a cement that binds society together (the functionalist sociologists, for example), and so on. These were all markedly different interpretations and understandings of ideology, often with very little mutual agreement. However, what united them all was a recognition of the relevance and the necessity of the concept of ideology. Whether these theorists have subscribed to a positive, negative or neutral evaluation of ideology, or opted for restrictive or all-inclusive concepts of ideology, or developed materialist or idealist interpretations of ideology, very few major social theorists of the twentieth century have dismissed the entire concept as being analytically or heuristically irrelevant or flawed. With the development of poststructuralism this has dramatically changed. Poststructuralism represents the first truly sustained critique of de Tracy's legacy. To varying degrees, and for different reasons, poststructuralists have opted out of the ongoing discussion initiated by de Tracy and they typically reject the idea that a discussion of ideology is relevant to our attempts to understand the contemporary world. The general outline of the poststructuralist critique, for all the different versions of it that have been articulated, can nonetheless be summed up quite simply. Poststructuralists have argued that from its inception the concept of ideology has remained chained to the problematic humanist assumptions that motivated the Enlightenment. Given the poststructuralist critique of humanism, the idea that one can 'rise above all particular social perspectives and reach a non-ideological definition of the nature of man' (O'Sullivan, 1989, p. x) is thought to be theoretically barren and politically dangerous. Where the classic texts of poststructuralism often tread carefully in rethinking and problematising other stalwarts of the theoretical lexicon, ideology has come in for straightforward attack and blunt rejection. Deleuze and Guattari's remark in the opening pages of *A Thousand Plateaus* is indicative of this blatant poststructuralist rejection of ideology: 'There is no ideology and there never has been' (Deleuze and Guattari, 1988, p. 4).

The aim of this book is to explore the significance and consequences of the poststructuralist critique of ideology while avoiding such strategies of blunt rejection. The chapters that follow aim to explore the possibilities for a nuanced and subtle poststructuralist problematisation of ideology and also to explore the resources available within contemporary ideology theory for accommodating and/or responding to poststructuralist suspicions about the humanist assumptions that drive ideology theory. As such, the book is divided into two parts. The first part of the book consists of four chapters which share one common theme – the rejection of a naïve poststructuralist critique of ideology. In their different ways, all four authors explore the possibility of developing a viable concept of ideology or its substitute, which would go beyond traditional ideology critique and would at the same time preserve central postulates of poststructuralism.

Iain Mackenzie's chapter, 'Idea, Event, Ideology', presents the broad outline of an encounter between competing accounts of the nature of ideas and events and the theory of ideology. It is argued that we cannot fully understand what we mean by ideology if we do not first have a sure grasp of what we mean by 'ideas' and the things that ideas are said to represent, 'events'. Once the conceptual ground has been cleared in this way, one can see why poststructuralists would want to be suspicious of traditional forms of ideology critique, given that poststructuralists have a distinctive account of both ideas and events; but one can also see why it is possible to reconceptualise a poststructuralist account of ideology, using these distinctive conceptions of idea and event. Mackenzie argues that this transforms the common view that poststructuralist theorists simply reject ideology into the view that they reject ideology only when it is based on majoritarian conceptions of the idea and the event. The chapter concludes with the claim that this should dispel the common but false notion that poststructuralism lacks the conceptual apparatus required to engage in effective social criticism.

In the second chapter, entitled 'Ideology and Imaginary: Returning to Althusser', Caroline Williams argues that in the light of the poststructuralist attack, the concept of ideology can be rescued by returning to its structuralist roots and in particular to Althusser's later work. The chapter is divided into three sections. Sections one and two explore the indicators of ideology in Althusser's work – the first, epistemological, and linked to his project to develop a science shorn of all subjective reference; the second, political, and linked to the constitution of the social subject and the materiality of ideology's practices. The third section considers Althusser's later reflections on what he calls 'aleatory materialism' or a materialism of the encounter. It is argued that the theory of 'aleatory materialism' offers a way out of some of the problems encountered in sections one and two.

Robert Porter's chapter, 'A World Beyond Ideology? Strains in Slavoj Žižek's Ideology Critique', critically analyses the theory of ideology put forward by Slavoj Žižek. The author argues that there are two strains or tendencies at play in Žižek's theorisations: an affirmative strain that takes ideology critique to be ethically motivated and a negative strain that constantly challenges any affirmative gesture aimed at justifying ideology critique. The chapter analyses the tensions between these two strains of Žižek's thought, and in the process provides insights into the idea of a world without ideology.

In the fourth chapter, 'City Life and the Conditions of Possibility of an Ideology-Proof Subject: Simmel, Benjamin and Joyce on Berlin, Paris and Dublin', Kieran Keohane discusses and formulates the revitalised urban spaces of Berlin, Paris and Dublin as ideological fetishes sustaining the consumptive desires of urban tourism and shopping as lifestyle. Benjamin's argument for the emancipatory potential in the outmoded commodity is disputed in the context of the reconstruction of the dead object as antique and thereby repository of the authentic, in the environment of postmodern nostalgic libidinal economy. The reconstruction of Dublin's Temple Bar as a 'cultural quarter' is similarly interrogated. Temple Bar is formulated as a simulacrum of modern urban street space, in which the conditions of possibility of the emergence of a prototypical utopian cosmopolitan subjectivity, exemplified in Joyce's Leopold Bloom, are being systematically eliminated. The persistence of social antagonism and the subversion of prevailing ideological interpellations in the postmodern urban environment are explored in all three cities.

The second part of the book is devoted to theoretical responses to poststructuralist attacks on ideology. The four authors represented all explore possible ways out of traditional ideology critique and its heavy-handed emphasis on the Enlightenment-shaped belief in the existence of sharp distinctions between science and ideology, truth and falsity or reason and prejudice.

In his chapter 'Rehabilitating Ideology after Poststructuralism', Siniša Malešević looks at the analytical relevance of the concept of ideology in the wake of poststructuralist criticism. He argues that although poststructuralism rightly challenges the totalising ambitions of ideology critique, being focused exclusively on the Marxist understanding of ideology, it fails to account properly for the contributions of other theoretical traditions. Poststructuralist preference for the concepts of 'discourse' or 'meta-narrative' over that of ideology has been criticised as being too relativist and analytically insufficient for empirical purposes. The author argues that the concept of ideology can be rehabilitated by moving it from structure-centred approaches towards more agency-centred theories of ideology and by shifting the emphasis from the function to the form and content of ideology. It is claimed that the subtlety of micro approaches not only can better respond to the challenges of poststructuralist criticism but also can rescue and give a new life to the concept of ideology.

In 'The Dialectics of the Real', Diana Coole offers a provisional defence of ideology inasmuch as it is one element within a dialectical understanding of social life. Ideology is understood in this context as referring to ideas and practices which block communication, exploration and interrogation in order to sustain established limits, boundaries, interests and privileges. From this perspective it is claimed that dialectical and genealogical, deconstructive or vitalist positions have more in common than poststructuralists generally acknowledge. Coole argues that some of the poststructuralist criticisms made of ideology elide the case against Descartes and Kant with that against Hegel and Marx, leading to an unnecessarily hostile response to dialectics as a critical engagement with the real.

Michael Billig defends the concept of ideology from a psychological perspective. In his chapter 'Ideology, Language and Discursive Psychology', he argues that any theory of ideology needs a psychological dimension to show how people think, feel and act ideologically. Given the recent interest in linking ideology to discourse, ideology needs a discursive psychology, which shows how psychological states can be constituted through discourse. It is suggested in this chapter that such a discursive psychology needs to take into account three psychological levels: conscious, preconscious and unconscious. Ideology provides the means for conscious deliberation through the rhetoric of argumentation and ideological dilemmas. Preconscious ideology functions through the familiar but often unnoticed elements of social life. In discourse, dietic aspects of discourse frequently function at this level. With regard to the unconscious, it is suggested that repression is essentially a dialogic process. Through acquiring language we acquire the ability to repress, and this ability can be socially practised. In this way ideology is revealed both by what is habitually said, and just as important, by what is habitually left unsaid.

Foucault

In the last chapter, 'The Birth of the Subject and the Use of Truth: Foucault and Social Critique', Mark Haugaard examines Foucault's concept of 'truth' and his declared death of the subject. While it is claimed that Foucault perceived himself as a radical philosophical relativist and that he was strongly committed to the idea of the death of the subject, it is argued in this chapter that neither are actually intrinsic to the logic of the theoretical position which Foucault develops in his genealogical histories. If one recognises, as Foucault did, that relations of domination are recreated through the reproduction of systems of meaning and reinforced through the language of truth production, one needs to know if this recognition is necessarily self-defeating. It is argued that Foucault presented his analysis in terms that have implications that are not inherent to such a perception of relations of domination and, furthermore, that the actual content of Foucault's genealogy offers evidence to support such a thesis.

All of these essays testify to the possibilities of a vibrant debate between poststructuralists and ideology theorists that does not necessarily end in unproductive claims and counter-claims. Although the mutual suspicion that exists between poststructuralists and ideology theorists will not evaporate overnight, this collection should serve to remind protagonists from both camps that the possibility of further discussion and debate exists in areas where even the most hardened battle lines have been drawn up. It is not clear where the debates between poststructuralists and ideology theorists will end up but there is reason to believe that ideology after poststructuralism will be marked by a new maturity that will enable de Tracy's brainchild to emerge from under the wing of an unsophisticated humanism.

REFERENCES

Deleuze, G. and Guattari, F. (1988) *A Thousand Plateaus: Capitalism and Schizophrenia*, vol. 2 (London: The Athlone Press).

de Tracy, A.L.C.D. (1826–27) *Éléments d'idéologie – l'Idéologie* (Brussels: A. Wahlen).

O'Sullivan, N. (ed.) (1989) *The Structure of Modern Ideology* (Aldershot: Edward Elgar).

PART I

Poststructuralism vs. Ideology

1   Idea, Event, Ideology

Iain MacKenzie

As the Paris uprisings of May 1968 summoned the dormant forces of backlash and reaction, from both Left and Right, Henri Lefebvre sought to understand the multifaceted nature of this event, and of events in general. He begins with the claim that events challenge the complacencies of those who concern themselves with, and find solace in, the world of ideas. Events, he says, 'pull thinkers out of their comfortable seats and plunge them headlong into a world of contradictions. Those who are obsessed with stability lose their smiling confidence and good humour' (Lefebvre, 1969, p. 8). This is a particular example of a general dogma – one that has currency both within the academy and in the world at large – namely, that the particularity of events disrupts the universality of ideas. Of course, in privileging the disruptive powers of 'the event' this dogma itself depends upon a system of ideas that posits the event as privileged. Generally speaking, one can call this 'background' reservoir of ideas the 'ideology' that motivates the analysis.

But if we define ideologies solely as sets of 'second-order' or 'background' ideas then this manoeuvre itself could be taken to task on the grounds that it idealises the concept of ideology. It could be argued, in fact, that such an idealist reading of ideology amounts to an *ideological* account of what is meant by the term ideology: ideological in that it surreptitiously and problematically privileges the realm of ideas over other realms. Although it seems intuitive to assume that ideologies are 'collections of ideas' that inform the way we look at the world (where 'the world' includes both ideas and events) there is an equally plausible counter-intuition that ideologies are at least as much 'collections of events' (where events should signify actions, practices, habits, etc.) that shape the world (again, where 'the world' includes both ideas and events). Given this, ideologies are not just collections of 'background ideas', they are also collections of 'background events'.

The same point can be made in a slightly different way. More than 30 years after the 'events of 1968', the turn to ideology is no longer a straightforward one. In the intervening years, an overly confident neo-liberalism (Fukuyama, 1992) and an extravagantly destructive postmodernism (Baudrillard, 1975) draped the intellectual skyline in a flurry of banners proclaiming 'the end-of-ideology' (while it was not the first time such banners had seen the light of day, the decay and eventual collapse of the Soviet bloc gave their message a new persuasive power). However, as the 'end-of-ideology' thesis is left in tatters – to the extent that it has been exposed as the ideological manoeuvre *par excellence* (for example, Derrida, 1994; Žižek, 1994) – the opportunity has now arisen for a new look at this seemingly withered concept (for example, Laclau 1996). As a result there has been a resurgence, albeit a cautious one, in the idea of ideology. A key theme in this new attitude of constructive interrogation, I would suggest, is a fresh look at what the theory of ideas has to offer ideo-logical analyses. One of the odd developments of previous, traditional, work on ideology had been its peculiar disregard for ideas. Indeed, this disregard became such a rallying cry that the theory of ideas, it seemed, had been overtaken by theories of ideology (a theme that will be taken up in the last section of this chapter). If this is to be remedied then the nature of the idea must be placed firmly at the heart of the nature of ideology.

But, as already stated, it would be foolish to subsume the theory of ideology within the scholastic world of the theory of ideas. This would inevitably result in a denigration of the 'active' dimension of ideologies; that ideologies have a role in shaping the world, not just a role in how we view the world, is poorly expressed solely as a function of 'ideas' (at least as we traditionally understand them). Freeden (1996), in one of the most significant contributions to the study of ideology in recent years, argues that it is misleading to view ideologies as pure systems of ideas. He argues, in contrast, that the most distinctive feature of ideological analyses is that they take ideas *and behaviour* into account (in contrast with the abstract approach of much contemporary political philosophy). As such, Freeden talks of ideologies as 'thought–behaviour' conjunctions (1996, p. 43). While this goes a long way towards capturing the complex nature of ideologies – that they are more than simply thoughts or ideas – throughout the discussion below I shall keep my distance from the concept of behaviour (which I understand to have a troubling ring of methodological individualism to it) in preference for the term 'event' (on the grounds that ideologies may shape the world in ways which cannot be accounted for by the idea of human behaviour). I take it, therefore, that ideologies are manifest not only as *ideas* in the world but also as *events* in the world. An ideology, one could say, is an idea–event conjunction. One cannot address the nature of ideology, in short, without implicating oneself in a discussion about the relationship between ideas and events.

Ideologies, then, are both ideas and events that shape the way we think about how ideas and events relate to each other. I shall outline below the various ways this knotty definition could be unravelled. In conclusion I shall propose what I take to be the only consistent way of understanding ideologies as both sets of ideas about ideas and events *and* as events which give shape to ideas and events. To do this I shall turn first to the nature of ideas, then to the nature of events before finally turning to a reconsideration of the nature of ideology.

IDEA

When one inquires about the nature of ideas one immediately faces a problem: how can one have an idea of ideas? But the problematic nature of such an inquiry gives the clue to how it can be overcome. Ideas have a mutually constitutive relation to problems, precisely because of the problem of finding an idea of ideas. We can understand the nature of ideas, therefore, by understanding how they relate to problems (whatever the problem, although ultimately the essential problem is always one of relating ideas to themselves). An investigation of ideas, then, requires an investigation of how ideas are generated in response to problems and how problems are generated in response to ideas. Of course, this is no straightforward matter. The history of philosophy is littered with attempts to cast this relationship between ideas and problems in the toughest metal, so as to avoid the corrosive powers of trying to generate an idea of ideas. I shall briefly outline five such attempts – those that I take to be the most dominant and the most revealing as regards the task in hand. In each case I shall associate the relationship between ideas and problems with a persona that represents the nature of philosophical activity implicit within the account. In addition, the problem of the political will be used as a way of indicating the nature of the idea at work in each account, an approach which also makes the transition towards the concept of ideology later in the chapter less of a jolt.

The five conceptions of the idea:

1. The problem is a poorly comprehended idea. On this account of the relationship between problems and ideas, we might say that the problem of the political is a result of a failure to comprehend

fully the nature of the political. The task of the philosopher in this instance is to reveal the true nature of politics such that, for example, politics is thought to be essentially the pursuit of justice. The philosopher, in other words, has a certain artistic role in that she helps us to comprehend the object, in this case 'politics', for what it really is. The persona associated with this conception of the relationship between ideas and problems is the artist.

2. The problem circumscribes the idea. On this account, there is not a failure of comprehension but a failure to state the problem correctly. One should not assume, therefore, that there is a nature of the political to be revealed. Instead, it is assumed that one can state the problem of the political in such a way that the boundaries of what might count as the political are properly demarcated. This leaves the nature of the political in a state of suspension and shifts the interrogative focus on to an analysis of the problem itself. The philosopher's role in this case is less that of the artist and more that of the artisan that helps to craft whatever idea we have of the political into a form appropriate to the problem of the political. The artisan, we might say, is less concerned with the nature of justice than with the right way to deal with competing conceptions of the nature of justice (or in a more contemporary vein, much recent political philosophy has come to define justice as that which mediates between competing conceptions of the good).

Both of these approaches assume that there is a certain timelessness about the relationship between problems and ideas. This is problematic to the extent that one takes as given the changing nature of problems, such that, for example, the political is thought to be a different problem at different historical moments (and, we must add, in different contexts). This gives rise to a strategy of making the problem of the political itself problematic. This strategy typically takes two forms, one which salvages the idea's relation to the problem and one which sets the idea adrift from the logic of the problem.

3. The problem is made problematic so as to pursue the logic of changing ideas. On this account the problem of the political can only be stated correctly if it is seen to be a problem that changes over time. In other words, there is no one way to circumscribe the political as a problem but a series of different ways which are then placed in relation to each other. The relationship between the idea and the problem is salvaged to the extent that one has an idea of the ways in which problems change. The philosopher in this case is not

the artisan who crafts our idea of the political into an appropriate form but an architect who builds the different conceptions of the political problem into a larger theoretical system, that is, one that harmonises the competing problems of the political into an idea of how the political may reveal itself by virtue of being placed in relation to other problems.

4. Problems and ideas are incommensurate. On this account, the historicity, and contextuality, of problems are seen to rupture any connection they might be said to have with ideas. The problem of the political, for instance, has no architectural resolution and this lack of resolution functions as the condition of the political itself. The political is defined by its very problematic quality and the world of ideas about the political is thought to be the very definition of the apolitical. Typically this account of the relationship is used to undermine all the previous accounts by dissolving them into variants of the first conception (that problems are poorly comprehended ideas). It nonetheless resonates with this very strategy to the extent that it depends upon an idea of the political as *essentially* problematic. One might say, therefore, that the philosopher in this instance, in trying so hard to distance herself from her role as artist, ends up playing the role of artist*e*; where the artist*e* is the mock artist, the one that assumes the garb of the artist in an attempt to lay bare the pretensions of the artist.

In summary, on the side of the idea we have the Platonic drive (1) to comprehend the essence of problems and the dialectical drive (3) to unravel the idea in time through problems. On the side of the problem we have the modern, typically Kantian, drive (2) to circumscribe the idea and the postmodern drive (4) to unhook the world of ideas from the world of problems. At this point one might be tempted to say that the logic of the relationship between problems and ideas has been exhausted. However, before giving way to this temptation it is worth inquiring further into the nature of this exhaustion. The solutions given to the relationship between problems and ideas are only ever partial solutions because they are predetermined by the way in which one constructs the relationship in the first place. Indeed, because of this, it is often thought that philosophy hits rock bottom and the analytical spade is forced to turn back on itself. The theoretical exhaustion arises, therefore, as a result of pursuing the impossible resolution of the essentially problematic. It is tempting to think, therefore, that one should make one's metaphysical choice and get on with the business of philosophy from whatever ground one has chosen. But, to the extent that this strategy is itself a resolution, one which is conditioned by a certain view of philosophy's relationship to the metaphysical (of the problem to the idea), the exhaustion that accompanies the initial conundrums will never be overcome. Perhaps this is why so much of contemporary philosophy lacks vitality; every intake of air serves to remind it of the exhausted state of its lungs.

Translating this into the realm of the political, it is sometimes said that one must plant one's feet in ideological soil in order even to enter the political arena. In other words, it is the very pursuit of an idea of the political in response to that which is perceived as the problem that generates the need for the concept of ideology or, putting it more strongly, the impossibility of escaping the ideological. This is problematic, however, to the extent that it treats the problem of the political as already given in the idea of the ideological: a relationship that can be played out in any of the four ways already outlined. At this point the metaphysical circles in which we are caught seem to take a distinctively vicious turn. And, for all that an increasing number of social and political theorists are trying to construct a 'politics' out of these disabling conundrums – witness the growing interest in 'the decision' as the formative moment of politics (Critchley, 1999; Laclau, 1996) – I want to argue that a more promising route can be taken by following through another way of conceiving of the relationship between problems and ideas. This leads on to the fifth option.

5. Problems and ideas are coextensive. We can say that on this account the problem of the political is that which expresses the idea of politics but that the idea of politics can only ever be expressed as a problem. The role of the philosopher on this account is twofold. On the one hand, the philosopher must reveal the partiality that will always haunt any attempt to resolve the relationship between problems and ideas. One can make the same point by saying that the task of the philosopher is to unmask the artist, artisan, architect and artiste in order to expose the prejudicial gaze that the mask is there to hide. On the other hand, the philosopher must turn this negative critique into a positive affirmation by conceiving of the problem as an idea. Here, one might say that the philosopher idealises the problem to the extent that she recognises the need to adopt a philosophical persona or mask. This seemingly contradictory gesture will flounder on the very same rocks as the other approaches if *one particular persona* is idealised in competition with

the others; that is, it will not escape the charge of predetermination – that one conceptualises the relationship between ideas and problems only by determining that relationship prior to one's 'solution' of it – if it is seen to give priority to a partial determination of philosophical activity (if under the masks of the other conceptualisations one is said to find the true face of philosophy). Therefore, we should think of the philosopher on this account as the one who constantly restages the relationship between problems and ideas without privileging any particular version of that relationship. The persona appropriate to this account is that of the person who adopts personas, the actor. In other words, the philosopher must 'act out' the resolution between problem and idea each time the relationship is 'staged' anew. Or, turning this passive construction into a more active one, it is through the various 'actings-out' that the very nature of the relationship is staged each time.

There is reason to believe that this is the least promising of all the options discussed so far. First, it may be said to dissolve the very distinction under scrutiny, the distinction between problems and ideas. Second, it appears to have compounded this by ignoring the conceptual benefits of historicising the relationship between problems and ideas. Both of these criticisms, however, miss the point. First, the claim that ideas and problems are coextensive does not dissolve the distinction between the terms; rather it makes the nature of that distinction relative to the event through which the distinction is 'acted out' or 'staged'. Political events, one might say, create a certain relationship between the problem and the idea of the political, such that they cannot be made subject to a predetermined sense of what constitutes the political in the first place. Second, the historicity of the relationship is to be found in the changing nature of events, rather than in a predetermined sense of what makes events change. The theatre of political events, one might say, is governed by the time of the 'eternal present', so long as one thinks of the present as that which lacks 'plenitude' and the eternal as that which lacks 'unity' (Foucault, 1977, p. 175). So the claim that ideas and problems coexist does not imply that the relationship does not change; on the contrary, it raises the possibility of real change, that is, change freed from a predetermined logic of change.

Both these responses, however, appeal to a logic of events that has yet to be fleshed out. Of course, the nature of the event, just like the nature of the idea, is one that is highly contested. It is important to consider, then, some of the different ways in which the event has been conceptualised in order to develop this discussion of the nature of ideas. In the process, the groundwork will be laid for the final section where I will show how this discussion of the idea and the event can be used to shed some light on the nature of ideology.

EVENT

It may seem odd to look to the nature of the event to bolster an abstract metaphysical claim about the nature of the idea. However, as I said at the outset, one cannot invoke the particularity of events without constructing an idea that governs that particularity. In other words, the world of events and the world of ideas are not mutually exclusive and antagonistic. Rather we should see events and ideas as constituting different dimensions of the same world. From this per-spective, therefore, it is important to consider the various ways in which these two dimensions may be said to intersect. This point of intersection we can call, in general, the sense of the event – the meaning the event has for us in constructing the problem and idea that we extrapolate from it. In politics this is clear: an event is made sense of in terms that establish a relationship between the problem of the political and its idealisation. For example, if the events of 1968 (which I'll be treating as a paradigmatic event throughout this part of the chapter) are made sense of vis-à-vis the failure (or not) of Left politics, then this in turn reinforces the idea that the problem of the political is one of class antagonism. So, to understand the different ways in which the event can be conceptualised we must think in terms of the relationship between the *nature* of the event and the *sense* of the event. With this in mind I shall now briefly outline a number of different conceptions of events and how we make sense of them. Each conception will be associated with a contemporary, broadly twentieth-century, school of thought, though this should not be taken to imply that the relationship between events and sense is a solely contemporary phenomenon (far from it!). I also recognise that the thumbnail sketches that follow cannot be said to capture the conceptual riches of each position. My aim is simply to map out a terrain of thinking about the event that enables me to make some general remarks about the relationship between ideas and ideologies.

I will examine seven approaches to the event.

1. *Positivism*. For the positivist the event is to be thought of as a transformation in a state of affairs such that the meaning of events, the sense we make of them, is to be treated as an attribute of that transformation. The events of 1968 are to be explained by reference

to the dynamics of French society and whatever sense is attributed to those events is contained within the explanation of that dynamism.

Now, the problems associated with a positivist logic of the event and its sense are well documented. Broadly speaking, positivism does not allow for the contingency of meaning that has become the bread and butter of contemporary philosophy. It lacks sensitivity vis-à-vis the mutable and contestable grounds of sense. This has led to a number of different approaches to events and their sense that reveal, to varying degrees, the shifting sands upon which we construct meaning.

2. *Phenomenology*. For the phenomenologist the nature of the event is located in material transformations but the sense of the event is to be found in the operations of consciousness. Much as for positivism, the events of 1968 are said to have a brute facticity about them but, in contrast to positivism, the meaning of those events is not contained within that facticity, rather it is found in the way the conscious subject signifies that facticity to itself.

3. *Structuralism*. For the structuralist the nature of the event and its sense combine in a logic of discursive transformation. The notion that events involve transformations is retained but the site of transformation is not to be found in the materiality of the event nor in consciousness but in the ways in which its sense is structured in relation to a field of signification. Typically, therefore, the event is a transformation in that field of signification, the discourse, rather than in the state of affairs that it may be said to represent. The events of 1968, for example, are to be understood in terms of the transformations and reverberations of this very phrase within and between discursive systems.

4. *Deconstruction*. The deconstructionist begins with the separation of facticity and meaning inaugurated by phenomenology and then doubts that the conscious subject can be said, in any foundational sense, to be the locus of meaning. Similarly, though, the deconstructionist doubts that one can straightforwardly invoke the discursive field as the locus of meaning. The consequence of this is a radical separation between facticity and meaning (where even the 'facticity' of the discursive field is rendered problematic). As regards the events of 1968, both the nature of the material transformation and the sense we can make of that transformation are held in suspension, such that all that remains is, in principle, an open-ended chain of signification.

5. *Hermeneutics*. From the hermeneutic perspective this radical separation of facticity and meaning goes too far. A relationship between the event and its sense, it is argued, can be established when one considers both aspects from an historical point of view. For the hermeneuticist, historicising facticity and sense usually takes the form of accounting for their split in terms of a narrative of cultural and self transformation such that we are in a position to assume their possible reconciliation. The nature of the events of 1968, in other words, will emerge in the process of trying to find the narrative that makes the most sense of those events.

6. *Critical theory*. Accepting the need to historicise the relationship between the nature of the event and its sense, the critical theorist nonetheless remains suspicious of the hermeneutic desire for a narrative of retrieval and reconciliation, arguing instead for a means through which the substance of such narratives can be assessed as reasonable accounts of the nature of the event (so as to avoid hermeneutics slipping into deconstruction). Putting it another way, reasonableness is formulated with particular regard to avoiding both the logic of the object so dear to positivism and the subjectivist baggage of phenomenology, the result being a stress on the inter-subjective, communicative, construction of reason. The nature of the events of 1968 is held in suspension until agreement is reached about the meaning of those events to all concerned (an agreement that is rationally grounded but sensitive to historical and cultural development).

In all of these cases, the desire to move beyond positivism has led to the creation of a certain distance between the event and its sense. This distance is problematic because it ultimately dislocates the grounds of sense from the world of events; one is understanding the event in terms not given by the event (consciousness, discourse, history, reason, and so on). Of course, for many that is the only option if one wants to escape the paralysing logic of positivism. There is one other option, however, that looks to salvage the positivist intuition that the event and its sense are bound together while retaining the post-positivist intuition that sense is changeable and contestable.

7. *Constructivism*. In contrast with positivism, the event is not simply a transformation within a state of affairs. Rather, the event expresses the transformation *between* states of affairs *in terms not given by* those states of affairs. Deleuze has given us a paradigm case of this when he contrasts the state of affairs denoted by 'green' with the

event expressed by the phrase 'to green'. As he puts it, the event should not be confused with 'the state of affairs denoted by the proposition' (Deleuze, 1990, p. 182). As he puts it in another text, 'pure events escape from states of affairs' (Deleuze, 1997, p. 21). While post-positivists assume, however, that this means that the sense of the event is given by reference to something beyond the event, the constructivist argues that 'sense does not exist outside of the proposition' (Deleuze, 1990, p. 21). For the constructivist, if sense resides anywhere other than in the proposition, anywhere other than in language, then one will never understand sense and language immanently.

But how can we think of the event as the moment of transformation between states of affairs *and*, at the same time, maintain that the sense of the event must be given immanently in language? On the face of it, this seems to cleave the event from its sense in the most radical way yet. However, putting it rather abruptly, exactly the opposite is true. If there were not transformations between states of affairs there would be nothing to sense to make sense. If things did not change, then we'd have nothing to say. Events are not separated from sense, therefore, rather events are the glue that stick things to words such that sense is possible. This avoids the pitfalls of positivism because it treats 'the glue' as made up of transformations, not given states of affairs, and hence it retains the post-positivist insight into the contingent nature of meaning. However, it also avoids the pitfalls of post-positivism by resisting the temptation to view this contingency in terms of external interference in the relationship between things and words. So, the constructivist maintains that sense resides 'on the surface' between things and words, where the surface is the event constituted as the moment of transformation between states of affairs.

Before turning to the nature of ideology, I will briefly comment on the relationship between ideas and events. As is well known, if the event is thought to contain and constrain its sense in the manner of positivism then the problematic nature of events is always already circumscribed by an idealisation of the event which renders it ultimately unproblematic – typically, in the name of 'common sense'. This is not the place to rehash the arguments against such a reductive move; suffice to say that, from a political perspective, the idea that philosophy is the mobilisation of a 'common sense' is incredibly dangerous as well as intellectually barren. But, if the event is separated from its sense, as a signification of something external to the event in the manner of *post*-positivism, then the problem of how to relate facticity and meaning will always be met by a solution that must be treated as ideal (the self, discursive structures, historical narratives, communicative reason or whatever). So, whereas positivism typically idealises the problem, post-positivism typically assumes an already idealised idea. In both cases, the issue of prede-termination, addressed earlier on, will always rear its head.

In contrast, if the event is that which makes sense possible in the first place then the problem of how to relate facticity and meaning is one that must be staged anew each time, with each event. As such, the meaning of events will never be given by reference to a prede-termined ideal of how sense relates to events. But, unless this passive account of the relationship between facticity and meaning is turned into an active one, it too will quickly become metaphysically exhausted. This active transformation requires divesting oneself of the tendency to think that events are things that happen which philosophers must make sense of 'after the event' and, instead, one must embrace the idea that philosophy is the construction of events. When we think of philosophy in these terms we can sharpen up the claim made at the end of the last section. Rather than say that ideas and problems are staged through events we should say that ideas and problems coexist in events.

IDEOLOGY

This chapter began with the claim that one cannot formulate an idea about the nature of an event without invoking an ideological frame of reference. I now want to examine how this general definition of ideology is affected by the previous discussions of the idea and the event.

One might be tempted to begin with a distinction between ideologies and the ideological, where ideologies are particular con-figurations of idea and event and the ideological expresses the inescapable fact that idea and event mutually presuppose each other. On this account, the task of the ideology theorist is to construct a graph of possible ideologies, with the points on one axis represent-ing the different conceptions of the relationship between problems and ideas and the points on the other axis representing the different conceptions of the event and its sense. One could then plot the various points and look for the regularities or irregularities that exist between these points. However, this image is deeply problematic, given what has already been said about the idea and the event, because it amounts to the claim that the idea of the ideological conditions the problem of how ideas and events relate, such that events and the sense we make of them are also conditioned by a pre-determined grasp of what counts as ideological. Given that this claim depends upon a certain constitution of the relationship between problems, ideas, events and their sense, it fails to grasp the essential contestability within and between all these terms. In short, this approach falls into the trap of predetermining that which it is trying to prove. If we blithely accept that the ideological conditions ideologies, the ways in which the idea and the event are combined, then we will plunge ever deeper into the metaphysical quagmire.

Traditionally this conundrum was simply ignored by jettisoning the problematic quality of ideas into a wilderness beyond the ideological. It was this I alluded to above when I suggested that ideology theorists tended to be wary of, even hostile to, the world of ideas. For many who study ideology it is precisely these disabling philosophical manoeuvres that lend weight to the fact that the study of ideology is first and foremost a sociological activity, where this is deemed to be the investigation of events with a more or less dispassionate and objective eye for the ideas that inform them and how they fit together (or not) – I say this aware of the fact that few sociologists interested in ideology are looking for 'objectivity' in their work. The problem is that no amount of trying to avoid the implications of these philosophical dilemmas – say, by framing the idea in given social conditions, or by trying to avoid any reference to one's social conditions by celebrating the inevitable contingency of it all – will ever truly sidestep the partial and problematic nature of an idea of ideology. Attempts to account for the nature of politics in terms of competing ideologies typically fall into the same trap – that is, predetermining the political field as already ideologically constituted so as to prove by way of an analysis of competing ideologies (idea–event conjunctions) that this is the case.

The issue at stake is this: even though particular conceptions of idea and event bring forth a concept of ideology, the ideological does not function independently of a particular conception of ideology. It is a mark of recent work on ideology, I would suggest, that it has tried to grapple with the fact that each configuration of idea and event posits its own conception of the ideological. Once this is accepted, the thrust of the discussion is led away from a configuration of the ideological as that which explains ideologies and towards a far less certain, but far more exciting set of possibilities.

One can take this notion further by clarifying that the distinction between those who espouse the ideological as the *condition of* ideologies and those who see the ideological as that which is *posited by* ideologies is not a distinction between a general account of the ideological field and a particularist rejection of that generality. The claim that each ideology posits its own conception of the ideological is just as general as that which takes the ideological as the condition of ideologies. However, there are different and competing generalities at stake. If the ideological is treated as the condition of ideologies then it functions as a given generality, whereas the claim that ideologies posit a conception of the ideological functions as an assembled generality that must be explained each time it is constituted. This is not mere sophistry; a given generality requires that the particular cases are subsumed within a logic external to the particulars, whereas an assembled generality views that logic as internal to each particular case. Of course, this distinction shifts the problem of the ideological on to a new level, which is not to say that one is trapped by this same problem but, hopefully, that one is moving closer to asking the right question. Indeed, the question we are now faced with is this: how can we explain the construction of internal, assembled, generalities about the ideological without reference to an external, given, generality that orders this construction? Broadly speaking, two answers have been given to this in contemporary social and political theory: (1) one that treats the assembled, internal, generality as given by a logic of negativity and (2) one that treats the assembled, internal, generality as given by a logic of positivity.

1. On this account the ideological posited by each ideology is that which the ideology itself can never explain. Because the metaphysical ground beneath one's ideological feet is essentially contestable, every attempt to construct an idea through its relationship to a problem and every attempt to make sense of events, carries with it the need to posit the ideological as that which lacks any fixity. This amounts to saying that the ideological is the moment of negativity within each ideology: every attempt to account for the relationship between ideas and events generates the possibility of saying 'no' to that relationship, even though this 'no' is solely, internally, conditioned by the idea–event conjunction in question (i.e. there is no way of constructing a total rejection of ideologies). The pay-off, it is argued, is that this negative construction of the ideological functions as a way of retaining the idea that one can, and must, in some sense, critique all ideologies by showing how they inescapably imply that

which they cannot explain. The generality of this claim is internal to the particular construction of each ideology because it shows that each ideological moment includes the rejection of the ideology which posited it in the first place. In the post-Lacanian work on ideology this is often described as the Real that is posited by particular ideologies but which forever escapes the attempt to account for it in the construction of the ideological.

The problem with this account is that it is hard to conceive of a moment of negativity that can be truly internal to the ideological field without it becoming a sham negativity, one that ultimately becomes an external general positivity, one that ultimately bolsters a certain idea of the ideological from an external point of view. Certainly, there is an avoidance of the straightforward 'givenness' of the ideological, but this only seems to hide a rather more surreptitious version which posits the 'givenness' of the negative as ultimately external to the ideological. In other words, it generalises the impossibility of a metaphysical ground as the very ground on which its analysis of the ideological is, paradoxically, made possible. Building on this idea, the critique of ideology that this approach is said to make possible will always be partial to the extent that it pre-determines the limits of available critical positions by fencing them into this account of the metaphysical. But if this is the case, and I grant that I have hardly shown it to be the case, then the second option needs to tackle head-on the pay-off presumed to reside within this logic of negativity; that is, the fact that it seems to make the critique of ideology possible. Does the second option address the internal nature of the general claim about the construction of the ideological while maintaining a sense that the ideological can itself be criticised (which after all would seem to be a prerequisite for avoiding the charge of predetermination, addressed throughout this chapter)?

2. On this account the ideological is that which engenders the need to constantly re-establish the link between ideas and events, on the grounds that an idea about an event only makes sense if one sees it as a problem. The difference between this account and the previous one is not always appreciated. The metaphysical ground is shifting, certainly, but this does not block the ideological completion of an ideology, rather, it requires that each time one links ideas and events, and thereby constructs an ideology of how they relate, one constitutes the ideological as that which makes it possible in the first place. So although these two options share similar theoretical

gestures the difference could not be greater – the one sees the ideo-logical as that which constitutes a lack within a given ideology, whereas the other sees the ideological as that which fulfils the rela-tionship between ideas and events. To reiterate: this can only avoid the pitfalls of the other approach if the idea is treated as essentially problematic (and the problem as essentially ideal) and if the event has its own logic of sense (not one given by another source). For example: the problem of the political is idealised by becoming that which is essentially problematic by the philosopher acting out the relationship afresh each time, a mode of philosophical inquiry that is given life by staging political events in such a way that the sense we make of it cannot be explained by reference to anything beyond the event.

What about the critique of ideology? The problem from a con-structivist point of view is that criticism often invokes a ground that is posited as larger than the grounded such that criticism 'serves only to justify traditional ways of thinking' (Deleuze, 1994, p. 153). The task of criticism, therefore, is to find a ground for criticism within that which one is aiming to criticise. This ground is exactly that which has been excavated through the discussion in terms of the principle that ideas and problems are coextensive in the event. The task of criticism, on this basis, is to create ideas, create problems, create events and to create sense where all of these terms are different dimensions of the same creative process. In this way one exercises the most devastating criticism that any ideology (and its correlative conception of the ideological) can face; one steps to the side of it and thinks differently, completely differently, about how ideas and events relate. One criticises a position as ideological, in other words, by refusing to occupy the terrain it has posited, though this itself can only be achieved by creating a new terrain of one's own. However, as this critique turns upon itself, the result is not the idea that all criticism must be ideological. Instead, we must conclude that all criticism is first and foremost creative and that the ideological emerges, precisely, at the moment when criticism stops.

This is sometimes taken to imply that one meets the claim that everything is ideological with the claim that 'there is no ideology and never has been' (Deleuze and Guattari, 1988, p. 4). However, the thrust of this discussion points to a different conclusion: forget all those slogans about the all-encompassing nature of ideology *and* forget all those slogans that urge us to forget ideology! Instead, construct the ideological every time one formulates an idea about an event in such a way that the ideological itself changes relative to the idea–event conjunction in question. If one can imbue this construction with a real vitality then one can become a real critic of ideology.

REFERENCES

Baudrillard, J. (1975) *The Mirror of Production* (New York: Telos).

Critchley, S. (1999) *Ethics-Politics-Subjectivity: Derrida, Levinas and Contemporary French Thought* (London: Verso).

Deleuze, G. (1990) *The Logic of Sense* (New York: Columbia University Press).

Deleuze, G. (1994) *Difference and Repetition* (New York: Columbia University Press).

Deleuze, G. (1997) *Essays Critical and Clinical* (Minneapolis: University of Minnesota Press).

Deleuze, G. and Guattari, F. (1988) *A Thousand Plateaus: Capitalism and Schizophrenia* (London: The Athlone Press).

Derrida, J. (1994) *Spectres of Marx: The State of Debt, the Work of Mourning, and the New International* (London: Routledge).

Foucault, M. (1977) 'Theatrum Philosophicum', in D.F. Bouchard (ed.) *Language, Counter-Memory, Practice: Selected Essays and Interviews by Michel Foucault* (New York: Cornell University Press).

Freeden, M. (1996) *Ideologies and Political Theory: A Conceptual Approach* (Oxford: Oxford University Press).

Fukuyama, F. (1992) *The End of History and the Last Man* (London: Hamish Hamilton).

Laclau, E. (1996) 'The Death and Resurrection of the Theory of Ideology', *Journal of Political Ideologies*, vol. 1, no. 3, pp. 201–220.

Lefebvre, H. (1969) *The Explosion: Marxism and the French Revolution* (London and New York: Monthly Review Press).

Žižek, S. (ed.) (1994) *Mapping Ideology* (London: Verso).

2   Ideology and Imaginary: Returning to Althusser

Caroline Williams

In his recent introduction to the collection of essays *Mapping Ideology*, Slavoj Žižek argues that the epistemological opposition between ideology and reality, on which the term traditionally relied, has collapsed. The tendency is for our theories of ideology to embrace and swallow even that 'extra-ideological ground supposed to provide the standard by means of which one can measure ideological distortion' (Žižek, 1994, p. 16). A crisis appears to pervade the concept of ideology, at least from poststructuralist quarters, but this crisis is not a new one. Since its inception, ideology has suffered from a lack of knowledge regarding its own limits. Finally to have absorbed the real is perhaps ideology's ultimate fate. Does this mean that the concept should be abandoned? Surely not – the title of this collection indicates that much. Indeed, Žižek also warns against the abandonment of the concept of ideology and proposes that we try to transcend this theoretical difficulty and maintain at least a political critique of the concept, form, and function of ideology. It appears then, that the concept must be salvaged from the reconfigurations in contemporary thought which sometimes seem to echo the 1950s chorus of 'the end of ideology'.

Why, nevertheless, return to an old structuralist, indeed one often accused of political dogmatism, a rigid theoreticism, an anti-humanism and a form of structuralism, all of which allow little space for the analysis of history and of the political, however we may wish to understand their inner dynamic? My reasons for returning to Althusser are many, and I wish to begin by setting out three of them. First, there can be no dispute that Althusser's work alone has had theoretical effects and consequences which he could never have anticipated. Althusser's symptomatic reading of Marx, his account of philosophy as a practice always linked to its political conditions of existence, and his radical and subtle account of ideology as an imaginary relation, travelled long distances towards sociology and political and social theory, along a route that also passed by gender and film studies, cultural and literary studies, as well as more obviously Marxist economics and radical philosophy. Michael Sprinkler (1995) points out that even amongst those who would now repudiate nearly every aspect of their Althusserian past, the occult force of Althusser's various indications concerning ideology persists. Every theory of ideology which takes its genealogy through Marx has also to pass by way of Althusser. Why is this the case? What is so distinct about Althusser's structuralist approach to Marxism and, more specifically, his reflections on ideology? Perhaps it is worth stopping with Althusser merely to recapture his theoretical and political predicament and to place it within our present theoretical and political landscape, a landscape marked by the challenges posed by *post*structuralism in particular.

My second reason for returning to Althusser is that his thought opens up many of the antinomies that have haunted, and continue to haunt, the concept of ideology. Some oppositions take us straight to the field of politics. In particular, oppositions between knowledge and mystification, power and subjection, theory and praxis. Others more clearly expose ideology's epistemological relation, namely, the dualisms between science (theory) and ideology, essence and appearance, objectivity and subjectivity, real and imaginary. Althusser spent his life pursuing this space of ideology suspended between politics and epistemology, indeed his writings show us that the two terms are inextricably bound. For Althusser, *there is no political conception of ideology that is not linked to epistemological concerns.* Perhaps it is the aporetic form of ideology, its tendency to wish for its opposite, truth, and yet always to be captured and distorted in political and social forms, that leads some poststructuralists, notably Michel Foucault (1980), to abandon the concept altogether. However, Althusser, and to some extent Foucault, stayed close to the problems pervading the concept of ideology wrought by its dual identity (at once political and epistemological), and continued to think through the dilemmas posed by the concept. One commentator has even gone as far as to say that the whole of Foucault's concept of discourse, most rigorously presented in *The Archaeology of Knowledge* is a dialogue with his former teacher Louis Althusser. At certain points below we will have the opportunity to consider the theoretical relation between the two thinkers (very often in the form of a dialogue without proper names).

The third reason for my return to Althusser's problematic of ideology (and its wider epistemological resonance) is generated by the more recent and provocative readings of his work. These readings are, in part, a response to the newly available posthumous notes and publications written by Althusser during his long stay in prison where his life ended. If we could agree that the author is a product of the interpretations which we (as readers) bestow on him/her then the Althusser of the 1990s is very different from the one created in the 1970s and 1980s. In fact I would go so far as to say that the former is a caricature of the thought of Althusser as it is presented today. This is not only because the readings are more nuanced and finely drawn than those previous discussions around structure and history, voluntarism and determinism, and associated centrally with the arguments of Anderson and Thompson. It is also because the later writings of Althusser expose the concern (already begun in his reading of Marx) with a theorisation of contingency and not a structural determinism (Elliot, 1998). Certainly these later reflections and insights were flashes of a new form of thought rather than anything systematically developed, but I am inclined to think that they may assist us in our discussions of ideology and indeed may give new form to Althusser's own 1972 definition of ideology as an imaginary, albeit wholly necessary, relation to reality. At the very least these later reflections may offer a response to some of the possible critiques of Althusser's somewhat antinomic rendering of science and ideology.

My chapter is divided into three sections. Sections one and two of the chapter will explore the two indicators of ideology in Althusser's work. The first indicator is epistemological, and linked to his project to develop a science shorn of all subjective referent; the second is political, and linked to the constitution of the social subject and to the materiality of ideology's practices. Section three will consider Althusser's later reflections on what he calls 'aleatory materialism' or a 'materialism of the encounter'. Here it will be argued that this form of materialism may offer a way out of some of the problems encountered in sections one and two. It may also, I will speculate, enrich Althusser's earlier, influential reflections on the concept of ideology (Williams, 2001).

IDEOLOGY AND SCIENCE

Althusser's quest to develop a science for Marxism may seem redundant today in light of poststructuralist critiques of the totalising tendencies of science. However this interest in a conception of knowledge which may escape all ideological form is central to many accounts of ideology, be they Marxist or other. For Althusser, the primary culprit, and the foundation of much ideological thinking, is the concept of the subject. In a statement which may appear to echo the position of the structuralist anthropologist Claude Lévi-Strauss, Althusser writes that 'it is impossible to *know* anything about men except on the absolute precondition that the philosophical (theoretical) myth of man is reduced to ashes' (Althusser, 1990, p. 229). His project, he writes in *For Marx* is 'to draw a line of demarcation between Marxist theory and the forms of philosophical (and political) subjectivism which have compromised or threatened it' (Althusser, 1990, p. 12). Thus begins Althusser's diatribe against all forms of Hegelian Marxism, notably that of Lukacs with its attendant historicism and humanism as well as its residual idealism, but also against many other forms of humanism, particularly the existential variety that remains tied to a conception of the subject as *cogito*.

Althusser's anti-humanist credentials are well-known. Less well-known is their source which must certainly be attributed to Spinoza rather than to Lévi-Strauss (Althusser, 1976, p. 132). In Spinoza, Althusser notes in a reflection omitted from his autobiography *The Future Lasts a Long Time*, '[I saw] ... the matrix of every possible theory of ideology' (Althusser, 1998, p. 7). 'Spinoza's theory', he writes elsewhere, 'rejected every illusion about ideology, and especially about the number one ideology of that time, religion, by identifying it as imaginary. But at the same time it refused to treat ideology as a simple error, or as naked ignorance, because it based the system of this imaginary phenomenon on the relation of men to the world "expressed" by the state of their bodies' (Althusser, 1976, p. 136). There is much in this reading of Spinoza that Althusser takes up in his political theory of ideology, but I want to focus, for the moment, on the problem of science in order to point to the significance of Spinoza's philosophy for Althusser's scientific epistemology and for his structuralism more generally.

There are three aspects to Spinoza's thought that are important to Althusser's epistemology. First, for Spinoza, the subject is not the primary object of knowledge; it is not even the creative agency of knowledge or a faculty of autonomous experience which, opposed to the object, creates the conditions of possibility for knowledge. Spinoza's anti-anthropomorphism precludes these forms of philosophical subjectivism. In fact, it is this denial of subjectivity and historical becoming or agency which was a source of criticism by

Hegel and others. 'The essence of man', Spinoza writes in *The Ethics*, 'is constituted by definite modifications of the attributes of God' (1992, p. 70). According to Spinoza, the subject is not the cause of itself, rather body and mind are different modes of existence of substance. Furthermore, and *contra* Descartes, body and mind are not perceived in a dualistic fashion where the first, through inward-turning (and, of course, a religious guarantee) can free itself from the passions of the body. For Spinoza, the kind of knowledge built upon such dualisms is one which gives full power to the imagination. It is unable to understand *the mode through which an idea and its corresponding object is constituted.* There is always an interconnectedness of mind and body, that which commentators have variously called a 'parallelism' or a 'symphony' rather than a dualism (Deleuze, 1988, p. 126). Crucially, the mind is an individual subject only because it is also a particular idea of the body (that is, the body is the material site of ideas). This does not however mean that the order of ideas in the mind and the body are adequate and clear; they may be imaginary, confused and fragmented, based solely on abstractions of the mind (idealism) or of the senses (a stark empiricism).

Secondly, Spinoza recognises three gradations in the form of knowledge that are replicated in Althusser's own conception of knowledge (see below). The first is derived from casual, subjective experience. Both Spinoza and Althusser would view empiricism as producing an imaginary – for Althusser, an ideological – form of knowledge because it takes the subject's experience and perception of objects as the basis for knowledge. The second form of knowledge is that based on common notions, or symbols that we come to associate with certain ideas and affects. Here the imagination is not a site of creativity and reflection as it will be in some later philosophies; the imagination distorts and confuses relations between things. For Spinoza, our moral distinctions and the imperatives which follow from law have their source in the imagination: order, goodness and beauty are deducible from nothing other than the affects generated by the imagination. This second kind of knowledge can nonetheless provide a bridge between the first and the third kind of knowledge. Common notions are evidence that thought is able to present generalities that are not founded upon the immediate experience of the body. Common notions illustrate the interconnectedness, the necessary integrations and classifications, that derive from the mind's ability to reason and understand the unity of affects of different bodies. It is only by thinking *through* the body that common notions can be derived. Spinoza calls this capacity of thought to think intuitively 'intellect', and it is the basis for the third form of knowledge. Significantly, it does not bypass the body because both mind *and* body are attributes of Substance and thus contain (modally) the conditions for reflexive, immanent knowledge (Lloyd, 1996).

The third and final aspect of Spinoza's thought which is important for the argument here is his concept of *idea*. Althusser drew upon this in his own epistemology and it represented, for him, a way of escaping ideological or imaginary forms of knowledge in order to develop a *scientific* knowledge of the third kind. For Spinoza, the construction of knowledge does not seem to require the existence of objects. *The idea comes before the object for Spinoza.* In what Althusser views as a fundamental attack upon empiricist conceptions of knowledge, and one which parallels his own critique conducted in *Reading Capital*, Spinoza makes an important distinction between the idea of an object generated through bodily affects and the idea of an object in thought. Thus, in *Reading Capital* Althusser writes:

> ...Spinoza warned us that the *object* of knowledge or essence was in itself absolutely distinct and different from the real object, for, to repeat his famous aphorism, the two objects must not be confused: the *idea* of the circle, which is the *object* of knowledge must not be confused with the circle, which is the *real object*. (1979, p. 40)

Knowledge is produced, then, according to conditions internal to its own production.

It is important to emphasise (although I don't think that Althusser took this wholly on board in his early adoption of Spinoza) that Spinoza does not develop an a priori conception of substance. This conception of knowledge is based on immanence, and not the transcendence of the world. There is no simple causal relationship between knowledge and world. Certainly, the order and connection of ideas is the same as the order and connection of things. Both are modes of being of Substance but the contingent, finite nature of mind and body, thought and experience, allows for the development of a kind of knowledge that always remains embedded in concrete life. In this way, Spinoza's Substance ('God *sive* Nature') functions as an absent cause with no absolute power of determination.

Althusser claims to find in Spinoza the resources for an autonomous conception of science that can distinguish itself from imaginary, ideological forms of knowledge. All empiricist conceptions of knowledge are to be rejected, even the more sophisticated, dialectical ones that posit a duality between the distorted world of appearances and its hidden essence, a duality that can ultimately be overcome. For Althusser, the division between fiction and truth, between ideology and the real, *are wholly internal to ideology*. Empiricist forms of knowledge impart a distinction *within* the real itself: 'it [the real] is structured as a dross of earth containing inside it a grain of pure gold, i.e. it is made of two real essences, the pure essence and the impure essence, the gold and the dross' (1979, p. 36). All that is required for knowledge to be unearthed, according to empiricist method, is for the real essence of the object to be dislodged from the impure dimension of the object. The grain of knowledge unearthed, however, is *already present within the object*. The formation or structure of knowledge here requires no separation or dislocation from the ideological impurities of the object, because the object of knowledge is intrinsic to the real, empirical object.

There must be a reframing of the problem concerning the question of knowledge, or as Althusser put it in an interview with Fernando Navarro, 'in order to change our world we must first change our way of thinking' (Althusser, 1994 and Navarro, 1998). It was a new apparatus of thought that Althusser intended to bring to Marxism by generating an epistemological break between the ideological and the latent scientism present in Marx, who did not have the conceptual resources to organise his work as a science. The aim here is not to open up old debates about the notion of a break (which one of Althusser's co-authors, Etienne Balibar (1996), has recently noted was more akin to an inner-theoretical tension than a clear demarcation). What is important to emphasise at this point is the way in which Althusser attempts to inaugurate a new mode of knowledge via a new way of understanding thought.

Nevertheless, this new scientific epistemology is not without its problems. Not only does the antinomy between ideology and science still appear in Althusser's formulation of knowledge, but it also makes it somewhat difficult to think their differentiation. Althusser does however recognise this problem: 'there is not one side of theory, a pure intellectual vision without body or materiality – and another of completely material practice which "gets its hands dirty"' (Althusser and Balibar, 1979, p. 58). Althusser draws upon Spinoza's account of three gradations of knowledge, where Generalities 1 corresponds to brute facts/objects; Generalities 2 to the field of concept production, the marking-out of a 'problematic' where, we may anticipate, ideology and science may intermingle; Generalities 3 denotes the space wherein a theoretical field of science asserts itself. Can these three regions remain distinct? If science is the *other* of ideology, then insofar as it tries to extricate itself from the clutches of ideology, it will be continually reinhabited and contaminated by it. This problem continues to haunt Foucault's *Archaeology of Knowledge* in the form of the opposition between the discursive and non-discursive realms, which only transcends the concept of ideology on the surface of things. Spinoza did not encounter such a philosophical antinomy between the imaginary and the true because he sought the transformation rather than the transcendence of the world of subjectivity. He thus established a parallelism between the order of ideas and the order of things and posited an interconnectedness between the imaginary and the true (or between ideology and science, to put the problem in Althusser's parlance). If this embodiment (without subjectivism) of science and ideology was established, it may save Althusser's epistemology from his critics who question the alleged containment of science from the world of ideology, and hence its divorce from any extra-theoretical referent. Before considering the moves Althusser made toward a rearticulation of this difficulty, let us turn to consider the more familiar terrain of Althusser's theory of ideology.

IDEOLOGY AND IMAGINARY

The later text of 1972, 'Ideology and Ideological State Apparatuses', rests, in my view, upon the prior epistemological work on ideology, even though the presentation of the problem is quite different. It should be clear from Althusser's critique of empiricism that a definition of ideology as an inversion, or mystification of the real, as presented (on Althusser's reading) by the metaphor of the camera obscura in Marx and Engels' *The German Ideology*, is rejected. Similarly, Althusser's rejection of the subject as the foundation, origin or essence of a theoretical concept precludes him from establishing an overly simplistic account of ideology as false consciousness, where the subject's experience of the world must become the source of knowledge necessary to transcend ideology. In his essay 'Ideology and Ideological State Apparatuses', Althusser is concerned *not* with an investigation of what particular subjects may think, or even *how*, by what means, they carry out the act of thinking, rather he is concerned with the *ideological mechanism* according to which thought, perception and subjectivity are produced. Althusser's central focus is upon the *representation* of ideology *within* consciousness, that is, the process by which the individual is constituted as a subject by ideology. Hence, ideology 'represents the *imaginary* relationship of individuals to their *real* conditions of existence' (Althusser, 1984, p. 36). Ideology then, is not to be associated solely with the realm of ideas; it is material and relational precisely because of its *structural existence*. Ideology is an element of the social totality and functions in a complex relation to the other elements or levels of the structure (for example, the legal, political, economic, cultural and philosophical and scientific levels). These levels are not hierarchical; there is no direct causality between infrastructure and superstructure. They are viewed by Althusser according to a model of *structural causality* which allows each structural mode a degree of autonomy from the rest, although it may in practice, under certain political and social conditions, become dominant.

Crucially, ideology has a material existence. Through its materialisation in state apparatuses, ideology can operate according to a number of different modalities. In his example of religion, Althusser notes the modalities of kneeling, the discourse of prayer, the sign of the cross, the gaze of the Absolute, all of which insert the subject into the materiality of religious ideology. Ideology appears to be at once a priori and timeless, in that it is a necessary structure which is always already regulated by ideological state apparatuses; it also has a specificity which allows it historical variance and a necessary responsiveness to particular political and social formations.

The concept of the imaginary is of central importance to Althusser's theory of ideology (as it was, above, in his theory of knowledge). It is, we might say, a foundational fantasy as the genesis of an experience of subjectivity which is at once primary, continuous and phantasmatic; it produces a structure of experience which is akin to what Ernesto Laclau (1996) has called, with a broader reference to the productive mechanism of ideology, a *constitutive distortion*, and it generates an account of the subject wherein ideology and subjectivity are inseparable. Althusser's concept of the imaginary is invested with allusions to Spinoza and to the psychoanalyst and philosopher, Jacques Lacan. From Spinoza, Althusser takes the view of the imagination as a source of deception and illusion; from Lacan, the view that the imaginary is a necessary form of misrecognition.

It deceives subjects as to their relation to the symbolic social order, the place of the Law and the only possible place for speaking and acting subjects. According to Lacan, however, the imaginary only partially constitutes the subject with a fantasy of wholeness and containment. It leaves a dimension of experience, the *real*, which is forever foreclosed and cannot be represented in the symbolic social order except through its effects. Althusser's theoretical explanation for this process of constitution is the much more inclusive notion of *interpellation*. This is the *structure of recognition* by which the 'concrete individual' finds its place and in doing so becomes a subject. The theory of interpellation performs a vital function of identification for Althusser, enabling subjects to recognise themselves in the dominant ideology. That such a structure of recognition remains forever on the level of misrecognition is a necessary and essential counterpart to the receipt of consciousness, belief, action and speech by the subject. In this way, *méconnaissance*, or the imaginary structure of ideology, is constitutive of the subject without remainder or residue.

I would like to spend the remainder of this section drawing out some of the criticisms of Althusser's conception of ideology; I will focus upon two criticisms in particular, (1) the form of interpellation and (2) the constitution of the real. In doing so I also hope to illustrate how Foucault's position is opened up within the Althusserian problematic.

The most repetitive criticism levelled at this conception of ideology is that the constitution of the subject as subjected being is absolute. A single spectacle, a single event of constitution, and subjects seem to work, in Althusser's words, 'all by themselves'. Whilst it is clear why Althusser wants to protect his analysis from the risks of subjectivism, this anti-humanist theoretical manoeuvre stops short of an analysis of exactly how material practices constitute particular forms of subjectivity, that is, the degree to which they succeed in their task of normalising and disciplining individuals. Some may recognise the seeds of Foucault's project in *Discipline and Punish*, which was influenced not only by Nietzsche's *Genealogy of Morals* but also, surely, by Althusser's 'Ideology and Ideological State Apparatuses'. What then of the problem of resistance, so central (if underdeveloped) to Foucault's analysis of power?

Althusser seems to assume rather than interrogate the sense in which the process of interpellation must be continuous if it is to produce and maintain self-disciplined subjects. There is no focus

upon the *perpetual* process of interpellation; no account of the link
between ideological state apparatuses and the constitution of the
subject, no reference to the role of linguistic articulation in the
theory of interpellation which can bring about the subject (i.e. 'It is
I, the subject of recognition'), and no consideration of the possible
relation between ideology and the unconscious. For Althusser, the
process of interpellation rests upon the singularity of the subject; it
submits to a logic of 'wholeness' and simplistic identity and, for some
critics, may even subscribe to a form of behaviourism. In other words,
the concept of the subject is not considered as a complex production
which is never fully constituted, thus always unstable and disruptive
of theories which retrospectively view it as such. This is precisely
where *Discipline and Punish* may exceed Althusser's formulations.
Whereas Althusser pushed the problem of the internalisation of
ideology to one side, preferring to consider the mechanism of interpellation as an imaginary recognition or a *méconnaisance*, Foucault
explores the physical processes of subjection, the way in which the
subject inscribes within itself the principle of subjection, and the
body as a transmogrifying site of disciplinary power.

I want now to turn to the second, thorny problem of the apparent
dualism maintained in Althusser's work between science and
ideology. In the essay on ideology, this problem is hidden, because
Althusser is at pains to show that ideology constitutes itself and its
opposite on the plane of the real. Notions of truth and illusion,
distortion and disjuncture of experience, as well as contradiction,
are all sustainable by ideology. Certainly, a powerful, determining
structure of ideology will mask and contain these divisions, but it is
significant that for Althusser there is no reality for subjects except an
ideological reality. This perspective is most difficult to marry with
the discussions raised in section one where there seems to be – at
least – a *potential* fluidity between ideology and science, imaginary
and true (real). For many commentators, however, Althusser
presents us with a rigidly structuralist conception of ideology which
reduces the subject to a mere function of ideological state apparatuses, together with an idealist conception of science that somehow
breaks with the ideological realm. Thus Derrida (1992) questions
whether both ideology and science may be 'cut off from their
history, from semantics sedimented within [them], as if one could
obtain a non-ideological, uncontaminated, scientific concept of
ideology'. Can Althusser move beyond this antinomy between
science and ideology?

IDEOLOGY AND (ALEATORY) MATERIALISM

I do not think that such interpretations of Althusser tell the whole story. Of course, discussions have now moved beyond this Althusserian problematic and we should perhaps be looking to those who have substantially developed his position, for example, Etienne Balibar, Antonio Negri, Pierre Macherey, as well as Foucault, and perhaps Deleuze (Stolze, 1998), for new theoretical directions. However, it does seem that in his later writings Althusser continued to think through the antinomies discussed here, and these must be sketched out. In *The Future Lasts a Long Time*, Althusser writes;

> In this fantastic philosophy of the necessity of the factual stripped of every transcendent guarantee (God) or transcendental guarantee (The 'I think'), I rediscovered one of my old formulas. I thought, then, using a metaphor – for what it's worth – that an idealist philosopher is like a man who knows in advance both where the train he is climbing onto is coming from *and* where it is going: what is its station of departure and its station of destination (or again, as for a letter, its final destination [an allusion here to Lacan and Derrida?]). The materialist, on the contrary, is a man who takes the train in motion (the course of the world, the course of history, the course of life) but without knowing where the train is coming from or where it is going. He climbs onto a train of chance, of encounter, and discovers in it the *factual* installations of the coach and of whatever companions he is *factually* surrounded with, of whatever the conversations and ideas of those companions and of whatever language marked by their social milieu they speak. (1998, p. 13)

It is through this metaphor of a train in motion that Althusser draws attention to a form of materialism that he calls *aleatory*: the materialism of the encounter. With this formulation all reductionist interpretations of Althusser as a structuralist who analyses formal rules of social formations in a trans-historical manner can be contested. What exactly is aleatory materialism? In this concept Althusser traces a path beginning with Epicurus, that is with the image of a disorderly fall of atoms through a vacuum causing their free encounter in order to give birth to a world. This materialism extends in a subterranean philosophical tradition from Lucretius to Hobbes and Spinoza, to Marx and Nietzsche, Heidegger and some of

Althusser's French contemporaries. Althusser referred, for example, to the materiality of the trace and invoked Derrida's analysis of writing and the trace as *différance* (Navarro, 1998). This material encounter is an ontological becoming but one without origin; it is ateleological but must not be viewed simply as a random, chaotic sense of historical temporality. It is also nominalist; it is always tied to particular cases because there exist, for Althusser, only particular cases, situations and events. Aleatory materialism is always, as Negri (1996) puts it, aleatory 'after the fact'. Thus every historical event must be understood as an exception; there can be no norms because every historical situation is underdetermined and therefore not wholly explicable in terms of a model. In other words, what Althusser sought to invoke was the thought of the new in the absence of determining conditions.

I will leave to one side the question of whether the structural/ scientific framework of Althusser's previous theoretical analysis is completely reversed; where some see a break or a turn, in the Heideggerain sense, others prefer to see continuity. What is important, as Negri also reminds us in his reading of the later work, is that Althusser now begins to consider the question of *bodies* and their powers of thought and freedom in place of the individual subject. Now we seem to find Althusser thinking about reality in the manner of Spinoza. In other words, to think about the true, to acquire a knowledge of the true, requires that thought passes through the body, and through relations between bodies. This is the basis of Spinoza's philosophy of immanence, and the parallelism between ideas and things (and bodies). It is the fuller philosophical schema rather than an isolated part (i.e. the three levels of knowledge) that Althusser now embraces. Hence:

> That one can liberate and recompose one's own body, formerly fragmented and dead in the servitude of an imaginary and, therefore, slavelike subjectivity, and take from this the means to think liberation freely and strongly, therefore, to think properly with one's own body, in one's own body, by one's own body, better: that *to live within the thought of the conatus of one's own body was quite simply to think within the freedom and the power of thought.* (Althusser, 1998, pp. 12–13)

It is an encounter with the power of thought without conditions. Ideology and a knowledge of the true become gradations or regions of the real rather than sliding into metaphysical dualisms.

What does this notion of aleatory materialism bring more specifically to the conception of ideology discussed in section two? On one level nothing seems to change. Ideology and power have achieved a certain dominance over, and unification of, social life and communication. The material forms of ideology, varied and singular as their modalities may be, have permeated the social body and rendering it a passive and inert subjectivity. With Spinoza, and to some extent after Foucault, thought must begin with the body, with the immediately lived relation to ideology, imaginary as it may be. Only then can its fissures and incompleteness be understood. It is surely to the dynamic, open, multiple and aleatory nature of the subject that Althusser's materialism points. Perhaps now, in the later Althusser, we find a means of understanding, and gaining a knowledge of ideology in terms of its effects ceaselessly to encounter and colonise a radically open form of subjectivity.

REFERENCES

Althusser, L. (1976) *Essays in Self-Criticism* (London: New Left Books).

Althusser, L. (1984) 'Ideology and Ideological State Apparatuses (Notes towards an Investigation)' in *Essays on Ideology* (London: Verso).

Althusser, L. (1990) *For Marx* (London: Verso).

Althusser, L. (1994) *Sur La Philosophie* (Paris: Gallimard).

Althusser, L. (1998) 'The Only Materialist Tradition, Part I: Spinoza' in Montag and Stolze (eds) *The New Spinoza* (Minneapolis: Minnesota University Press).

Althusser, L. and Balibar, E. (1979) *Reading Capital* (London: Verso).

Balibar, E. (1996) 'Structural Causality, Overdetermination, and Antagonism' in Callari and Ruccio (eds) *Postmodern Materialism and the Future of Marxist Theory: Essays in the Althusserian Tradition* (Hanover, NH: Wesleyan University Press).

Deleuze, G. (1988) *Spinoza: Practical Philosophy* (San Francisco: City Lights Books).

Derrida, J. (1992) 'Politics and Friendship' in Kaplan and Sprinkler (eds) *The Althusserian Legacy* (London: Verso).

Elliott, G. (1998) 'The Unknown Althusser' *Radical Philosophy*, no. 90.

Foucault, M. (1980) 'Truth and Power' in Gordon (ed.) *Power/Knowledge: Selected Interviews and Other Writings, 1972–77* (Brighton: Harvester Press).

Laclau, E. (1996) 'The Death and Resurrection of the Theory of Ideology', *Journal of Political Ideologies*, vol. 1, no. 3, pp. 201–220.

Lloyd, G. (1996) *Spinoza and the Ethics* (London: Routledge).

Navarro, F. (1998) 'An Encounter with Althusser' *Rethinking Marxism*, vol. 10, no. 3.

Negri, A. (1991) *The Savage Anomaly: The Power of Spinoza's Politics* (Minneapolis: Minnesota University Press).

Negri, A. (1996) 'Notes on the Evolution of the Later Althusser' in Callari and Ruccio (eds) *Postmodern Materialism and the Future of Marxist Theory: Essays in the Althusserian Tradition* (Hanover, NH: Wesleyan University Press).

Spinoza, B. (1992) *Ethics* (Indianapolis: Hackett Publishing Co.).

Sprinkler, M. (1995) 'The Legacies of Althusser' in Lezra (ed.) *Depositions: Althusser, Balibar, Macherey and the Labour of Reading* (New Haven: Yale University Press).

Stolze, T. (1998) 'Deleuze and Althusser: Flirting with Structuralism' *Rethinking Marxism*, vol. 10, no. 3, pp. 51–63.

Williams, C. (2001) *Modern French Philosophy: Modernity and the Persistence of the Subject* (London: Athlone Press).

Žižek, S. (1989) *The Sublime Object of Ideology* (London: Verso).

Žižek, S. (1994) 'The Spectre of Ideology' Introduction to Žižek (ed.) *Mapping Ideology* (London: Verso).

3   A World Beyond Ideology? Strains in Slavoj Žižek's Ideology Critique

Robert Porter

The intention in this chapter is to explore Slavoj Žižek's concept of ideology critique. But before doing this we will need to find a way of animating and framing the terms on which our discussion will proceed. We can begin by briefly calling upon a fragment of a story from Paul Auster's novel *The New York Trilogy*. Daniel Quinn, a writer of detective novels, finds himself in the strange and somewhat ironic situation of acting as a real detective tracking Peter Stillman. Stillman is a man consumed by the desire to seek communi(cati)on with God; that is to say, he is convinced that he can reverse the 'fall of man' by positively appropriating or 'speaking God's language' (Auster, 1992, p. 49).

For Stillman, humanity needs to move beyond the 'brokenness' of a world distorted by falsifying symbols to an ordered universe restored to wholeness: a world in which 'words' and 'things' come together in true reciprocity. His task, he tells Quinn, is to invent a 'new language':

> that will at last say what we have to say. For our words no longer correspond to the world. When things were whole, we felt confident that our words could express them. But little by little these things have broken apart, shattered, collapsed into chaos. (Auster, 1992, p. 77)

Stillman's desire to restore the 'world' and 'words' to one ordered 'whole' assumes a concrete horror for his son who is subjected to a most ghastly experiment. He imprisons his two-year-old boy for nine years, locking him up in a darkened room devoid of any human or communicative contact. Why? Stillman believed that his son would be open to the possibility of speaking the language of God if he remained untainted by the distortions and falsifications supposedly inherent in the symbols of modern everyday speech.

Peter junior tells Quinn the story retrospectively in his own peculiar form of words:

> So I am telling you about the father. It is a good story, even if I do not understand it. I can tell it to you because I know the words ... The father talked about God. He wanted to know if God had a language. Don't ask me what this means. I am telling you because I know the words. The father thought a baby might speak if it saw no people. But what baby was there? Ah. Now you begin to see ... Of course, Peter knew some people words. That could not be helped. But the father thought that maybe Peter would forget them. After a while. That is why there was so much boom, boom, boom. Every time Peter said a word, his father would boom him. At last Peter learned to say nothing. Ya ya ya. Thank you. (Auster, 1992, p. 20)

In what way, then, does this fragment of Auster's writing help us in framing our exploration of Žižek's notion of ideology critique? The first point to be made is that Stillman is actually engaged in a critique of ideology. That is to say, he is concerned with developing and maintaining a critical distance from the ideology he encounters in the social field (a world of distorting and falsifying symbols, a world in which words and things have become detached from one another). One of the most significant aspects of this critical gesture is that it is ethically motivated. Stillman is disgusted and dismayed by the moral fragmentation and anomie he finds in the world ('things have broken apart, shattered, collapsed into chaos', etc.) and he seeks ethical transcendence in God's word (the 'new language that will at last say what we have to say').

The problem, of course, is that Stillman's ethic institutionalises a new, and rather violent, ideology of its own. This, clearly, can be seen in his treatment of Peter junior, for the boy is treated as a mere instrument to be employed in the pursuit of God's word. This brings into focus a point that will prove to be important from a Žižekian perspective: namely, that the notion of experiencing an ethic beyond ideology (God's language beyond falsifying everyday speech, etc.) is always precarious because the subject (Stillman) who posits this ethic may remain pathologically or, as Žižek would say, *psychotically distanced* from the negative and repressive consequences that follow from its realisation (Žižek, 1989, pp. 165–166).

Perhaps now we are in a position to begin framing the terms on which we will explore Žižek's concept of ideology critique. The following points, implied by what we have already said, also anticipate and rely on Žižekian arguments that will be encountered as our discussion unfolds. Firstly, and most obviously, critique involves maintaining a distance between ideology and non-ideology. Secondly, this critical gesture is ethically motivated. Thirdly, the subject's experience of an ethic beyond ideology is always precarious, defined, as it can be, in negative terms: that is, by what it lacks, by the way in which it is limited and repressive. Put more broadly, then, we could suggest that there are two *strains* or tendencies at play in Žižek's theorisation of ideology critique. Firstly, there is an *affirmative strain* in the sense that ideology critique is ethically motivated, concerned with positively justifying itself in moral terms. Secondly, there is a *negative strain* in the sense that ideology critique bears witness to the negative possibility that the terms of its justification can be antagonistically challenged, revealed as limited, lacking, etc.

In the first part of the chapter we will focus on the negative strain in Žižek's ideology critique. That is to say, we shall witness the way Žižek, in a quasi-Lacanian fashion, relates the idea of negativity to the notion that we can take a critical stand against ideology. In the second part of the chapter we will focus on the affirmative strain in his critical thinking. That is to say, we will see that the ethical motivation to engage in ideology critique involves, Žižek says in a quasi-Kantian fashion, the affirmation of universality and moral responsibility. It will be the aim of our conclusion to think through the way in which Žižek theoretically relates these (negative and affirmative) tendencies and briefly to make some critical remarks about the consistency he lends to them. Also, we shall consider how these strains of Žižekian thought may help us evaluate the notion that we can experience a world beyond ideology.

IDEOLOGY CRITIQUE AND NEGATIVITY

We implied above that Žižekian critique involves maintaining a distance between ideology and non-ideology. But how is this to be done? We can look to the Introduction of *Mapping Ideology* for a sense of how this issue is played out in Žižek's thought (Žižek, 1994, pp. 1–33). Žižek begins his remarks by posing a question. He asks: 'Critique of Ideology, today?' What does Žižek mean by posing this question? Perhaps he is saying that dismissive criticism of the concept of ideology is rendered problematic by our seemingly irreducible experience of it in the contemporary political arena. So the accent on the question would be one of surprise, perhaps even disdain. 'You mean to critically dismiss the concept of ideology', we could imagine Žižek saying, 'when ideologues all around us continue to work their magic?' This stress on the continuing importance of the play of ideology in the contemporary political arena is made explicit when Žižek writes:

> it seems easier to imagine the end of the world than a far more modest change in the mode of production, as if liberal capitalism is the 'real' that will somehow survive even under conditions of a global ecological catastrophe ... One can thus categorically assert the existence of ideology qua generative matrix that regulates the relationship between visible and non-visible, between imaginable and non-imaginable, as well as the changes in this relationship. (Žižek, 1994, p. 1)

We can begin to give further sense to Žižek's categorical assertion concerning the 'existence of ideology qua generative matrix' regulating the 'visible and non-visible', 'imaginable and non-imaginable', by referring briefly to certain scenes from D. H. Lawrence's *Women In Love*. Consider, in the first instance, the following conversation between Gerald Crich and Rupert Birkin:

> 'And we've got to live for *something*, we're not just cattle that can graze and have done with it', said Gerald.
> 'Tell me,' said Birkin, 'What do you live for'?
> Gerald's face went baffled.
> 'What do I live for?' he repeated. 'I suppose I live to work, to produce something, in so far as I am a purposive being. Apart from that, I live because I am living.'
> 'And what's your work? Getting so many more thousands of tons of coal out of the earth every day. And when we've got all the coal we want, and all the plush furniture, and pianofortes, and the rabbits are all stewed and eaten, and we're all warm and our bellies are filled and we're listening to the young lady performing on the pianoforte – what then?' (Lawrence, 1996, p. 72)

Gerald's ideology is assembled according to an ethos of capitalist productivity. His position or social standing – as an industrialist or coal magnate – is mocked by Birkin who clearly is seeking to push beyond the limits of the bourgeois order – the world of desiring 'plush furniture' and 'pianofortes' etc. – in which his friend is implicated. The critical and caustic question – 'what then?' – strains at the teleology of a capitalistic desire – to produce and consume – by rendering *visible* or *imaginable* certain alienating consequences that flow from its realisation. To put it another way, the generative ideological matrix at play in Gerald's ethos of capitalist productivity, for Birkin, cannot render 'invisible' or 'non-imaginable' the consumptive and ideological limits it imposes on subjects who must, in order to accumulate goods, labour in the most mechanical, horrible and alienating conditions. Birkin confronts Gerald:

> 'We are such dreary liars. Our one idea is to lie to ourselves. We have an ideal of a perfect world, clean and straight and sufficient. So we cover the earth with foulness; life is a blotch of labour, like insects scurrying in filth, so that your collier can have a pianoforte in his parlour, and you can have a butler and a motor-car in your up-to-date house .... (Lawrence, 1996, p. 71)

This, of course, is not to say Birkin is beyond reproach from an ideological point of view. There is a tendency for Birkin to lapse into what we could, in Deleuze's Nietzschean terms, call a *negative nihilism* that judges social life in accordance with 'superior' values which, in actuality, are themselves abstracted from life (Deleuze, 1986, p. 147). We can detect this in Birkin's desire to replace the life or social fabric of the bourgeois world with, what he dramatically terms, 'the finality of love'. Birkin says:

> 'The old ideals are dead as nails – nothing there. It seems to me there remains only this perfect union with a woman – sort of ultimate marriage – and there isn't anything else.'
> 'And you mean if there isn't the woman, there's nothing?' said Gerald.
> 'Pretty well that – seeing there's no God.' (Lawrence, 1996, p. 75)

Thus Birkin could be seen to be judging the world – the social relations and values that constitute the bourgeois order of industry, labour, production, consumption, etc. – while dramatically positing the superior value of a 'perfect union with a woman'. This ideology of love (as a 'sort of ultimate marriage') regulates, in Žižek's terms, its own zone of visibility/non-visibility, imaginability/non-imaginability in that it acts as a limit horizon with regard to the object of unification: namely, woman. It is no surprise that Birkin reacts badly to an actual – living, breathing – woman who critically questions his mystical ideology of sexual harmony and union. Consider the following exchange between Birkin and Ursula Brangwen:

> 'I do think', he said, 'that the world is only held together by the mystic conjunction, the ultimate unison between people – a bond. And the immediate bond is between man and woman.'
>
> 'But it's such old hat', said Ursula. 'Why should love be a bond? No, I'm not having any.'
>
> 'If you are walking westward,' he said, 'you forfeit the northern and eastward and southern direction. If you admit a unison, you forfeit all the possibilities of chaos.'
>
> 'But love is freedom', she declared.
>
> 'Don't cant to me', he replied. 'Love is a direction which excludes all other directions. It's a freedom *together*, if you like.'
>
> 'No,' she said, 'love includes everything.'
>
> 'Sentimental cant', he replied. 'You want the state of chaos, that's all. It is ultimate nihilism, this freedom-in-love business, this freedom which is love and love which is freedom. As a matter of fact, if you enter into a pure unison, it is irrevocable, and it is never pure till it is irrevocable. And when it is it is one way, like the path of a star.'
>
> 'Ha!' she cried bitterly. 'It is the dead old morality.' (Lawrence, 1996, p. 179)

Birkin is never more the reactive nihilist than when he accuses Ursula of 'ultimate nihilism'. His suggestion that her ideology of love – 'this freedom which is love' – is abstract and life denying clearly applies to his own discourse concerning the 'mystic conjunction' between 'man and woman'. Ideologically speaking, such a discourse desires to make 'woman' 'invisible', 'non-imaginable' – that is, as a critic, someone who questions, who talks back, etc. – by abstracting her from the world and supposedly joining with her in the 'stars'. There is, in Birkin's discourse, a kind of Schopenhauerian will to nothingness, a nirvana of what he calls 'mystic balance and integrity – like a star balanced with another star' (Lawrence, 1996, p. 179). Of course, Ursula, in critically suggesting that he is labouring under a 'dead old morality', is Nietzschean enough to recognise that all this talk still masks a will to order and judge her as a – critical, question-ing – woman living in the world.

Now, nothing that has been said so far concerning Žižek's 'cat-egorical' assertion of the 'existence' of the ideological – as that which limits the social field by regulating and institutionalising zones of visibility/non-visibility, imaginability/non-imaginability – would seem to support the view that he wants to maintain a critical distance between ideology and non-ideology. To put it in the form of a question: can Žižek be thought to be holding out for a world beyond ideology while simultaneously positing, what he calls, 'the unrelenting pertinence of ... ideology' (Žižek, 1994, p. 1)? The idea that we can move beyond or transcend ideology becomes problem-atic with Žižek in that it is caught up in the following paradox. As Žižek puts it: 'The paradox ... is that the *stepping out of (what we experience as) ideology is the very form of our enslavement to it*' (Žižek, 1994, p. 6).

Stillman senior desired to step out of an experience of 'chaos' in a fallen world through ascension and the assumption of the language of God. He becomes entranced by this ideology of ascension and consequently institutionalises a zone of the non-visible; a non-visibility which takes on a horrifyingly literal meaning for his son who is banished to a darkened world without human contact. Birkin, to take another example, wants to move beyond or step out of a capitalistic ethos of production and consumption. In its stead, though, he labours under an ideology of love (love as mystical conjunction and balance, etc.) that desires to render invisible or domesticate the living, and critically questioning, woman (Ursula). To reiterate the Žižekian point: *both these cases presuppose a critical attempt to move beyond ideology that immediately and paradoxically ends in ideological enslavement.*

Yet, if we agree with Žižek that any attempt to move beyond ideology immediately and paradoxically involves our enslavement to it, are we not undercutting any possibility of justifiable critique? To put the question another way: how can a critic of ideology remain so if the very act of criticising itself is ideologically implicated? In these terms, the position of the critic, if (s)he is to remain free from ideology, would only seem to exist in the abstract; that is, removed from social life. Žižek is not unaware of this problem. He writes:

does not the critique of ideology involve a privileged place, somehow exempted from the turmoils of social life, which enables some subject-agent to perceive the very hidden mechanism that regulates social visibility and non-visibility? Is not the claim that we can accede to this place the most obvious case of ideology? (Žižek, 1994, pp. 3–4)

Yet, for all this, Žižek is absolutely insistent on retaining a critical-theoretical use for the notion of a non-ideological world or, what he actually calls, 'extra-ideological reality'. That is to say, he wants to insist that we can still maintain a critical distance from ideology. It is worth quoting him at length here:

> one should be careful to avoid the last trap that makes us slide into ideology under the guise of stepping out of it. That is to say, when we denounce as ideological the very attempt to draw a clear line of demarcation between ideology and actual reality, this inevitably seems to impose the conclusion that the only non-ideological position is to renounce the very notion of extra-ideological reality and accept that all we are dealing with are symbolic fictions – *such a quick, slick 'postmodern' solution, however, is ideology par excellence*. It all hinges on our persisting in this impossible position: although no clear line of demarcation separates ideology from reality, although ideology is at work in everything we experience as 'reality', we must none the less maintain the tension that keeps the critique of ideology alive ... ideology is not all; it is possible to assume a place that enables us to maintain a distance from it, *but this place from which one can denounce ideology must remain empty, it cannot be occupied by any positively determined reality* – the moment we yield to this temptation, we are back in ideology. (Žižek, 1994, p. 17)

It is clear from the above that Žižek expresses the intention to negate the ideological: that is, to use the negative in a critical stand against ideology. To put it differently, Žižek theorises the spatial position of the critic of ideology – the 'place from which one can denounce ideology' – negatively: as 'empty' or, more accurately, as an emptying of all and 'any positively determined reality'. Further, he is content, paradoxically, to recognise that such a theoretical under-standing of ideology critique makes him persist in maintaining a 'position' that is *impossible*. In these speculative and rather abstract terms: negativity is characterised by its impossibility, by its failure to sustain itself in any positive determination. Or to make the point in the opposite way, any 'positively determined reality' has its being reflected in a failure to occupy the impossible place of the negative. Žižek, of course, uses the Lacanian idea of the 'Real' to approach this negative idea of an impossibility that gives rise to failure. He writes:

> The Real is ... that which cannot be inscribed ... the rock upon which every formalisation stumbles. But it is precisely through this failure that we can in a way encircle, locate the empty place of the Real. In other words, the Real cannot be inscribed, but we can inscribe this impossibility itself, we can locate its place: a traumatic place which causes a series of failures. And Lacan's whole point is that the Real is nothing but this impossibility of its inscription: the Real is not a transcendent positive entity, persisting somewhere beyond the symbolic order like ... some kind of Kantian 'Thing-in-itself' – in itself it is nothing at all, just a void, an emptiness in a symbolic structure marking some central impossibility. (Žižek, 1989, pp. 172–173)

We can now begin to see the precise Žižekian terms in which Stillman's transcendentally motivated critique of ideology becomes problematic. In a sense, Stillman senior's belief in a pure language of God beyond the distorting and broken symbols of our fallen world expresses a desire for what Žižek above calls 'a transcendent positive entity, persisting somewhere beyond the symbolic order'. The problem with such a transcendental desire is that it is marked by a 'central impossibility'. This impossibility, we should say, is *purely* or *radically* insistent in that it is always *immanently* caught up in the *experience* of the critic (we could also think of Birkin here) who symbolically posits (for example, in the discourse of a mystical union between man and woman) a world beyond (bourgeois) ideology. That is to say, what Žižek calls the 'pure' or 'radical negativity' of the 'Real' acts as an 'immanent' 'limit' rendering 'impossible' the transcendental desire to purge the world of ideological configurations (Žižek, 1989, pp. 205–206).

Further, it should be stressed that the 'immanent' and radically negative 'experience' of the 'Real' is characterised by its *necessity*. Just as it is 'impossible' to 'occupy' the place or 'position' of the 'Real', it, according to Žižek's view, 'is even more difficult to avoid it' (Žižek, 1989, p. 155). That is to say, if we can never fully immerse ourselves in the 'Real', we simultaneously can never escape from it; that is, from the necessary failure caused by our attempts to symbolise it.

Such ontological necessity or cause expresses itself in a peculiar way: it is, in Žižek's words, 'a cause which in itself does not exist – which is present only in a series of effects ...' (Žižek, 1989, p. 163). Now, the political significance of thinking about the radical 'non-existence' or 'negativity' that defines the ontological necessity of the 'Real' is that it gives rise to a logic of *antagonism* which, as Žižek puts it, 'prevents the final totalisation of the social-ideological field' (Žižek, 1989, p. 164).

We can again use the exchange between Gerald Crich and Birkin discussed above to help us animate this Žižekian logic of antagonism. When Birkin questions Gerald's ideology or ethos of capitalistic productivity, he is, in Žižek's terms, pointing up the *negative* fact that the social reality implied by this ideology – a reality of purposive work, of production, consumption, etc. – *does not exist* in a self-enclosed harmonious way. That is to say, in critically suggesting that the bourgeois pursuit of material goods – 'cars', 'pianofortes', etc. – condemns many to a life of alienating work, Birkin, on Žižek's view, is rendering 'visible' or 'imaginable' certain impediments that could be used to challenge antagonistically the efficacy of ordering the social along capitalist lines.

Now, Žižek's point is that such antagonistic critique is contingent on the fact that a purely positive and self-enclosed social totality can never be institutionalised. It is always the case that posited ideological positions such as Gerald's are haunted by the 'Reality' of 'radical negativity': that is, by the spectre of disharmony and incompleteness (this, of course, is also implied in Ursula's antagonistic critique of Birkin mapped out above). Put speculatively: it is the constitutive incompleteness or lack inherent in the positivity of the social-ideological field that allows for the continuing antagonistic struggle that would challenge its foreclosure. Interestingly, these are the terms in which Žižek reconstructs the Marxian notion of 'class struggle'. He writes:

> [T]he ultimate paradox of the notion of class struggle is that society is 'held together' by the very antagonism ... that forever prevents its closure in a harmonious, transparent, rational Whole – by the very impediment that undermines every rational totalisation. Although 'class struggle' is nowhere directly given as a positive entity, it nonetheless functions, *in its very absence*, as the point of reference enabling us to locate every ... meaning ('transcendental signified') ... as (an)other attempt to conceal and 'patch

up' the rift of class antagonism, to efface its traces. (Žižek, 1994, pp. 21–22)

So we witness Žižek returning to Marx, but returning via a Lacanian detour. This 'return to Marx', he says, 'entails a radical displacement of the Marxian theoretical edifice' (Žižek, 1994, p. 28). The displacement, of course, is inevitable given Žižek's – Lacanian inspired – assertion of the constitutive incompleteness or lack inherent in any attempted foreclosure of the social-ideological field. Oddly enough, the theoretical-conceptual resources needed for a consistent recognition of this lack or failure are, according to Žižek, to be found in a thinker who Marx famously dismissed as ideologically conservative. This thinker, of course, is Hegel. Žižek writes:

[T]he most consistent model ... of antagonism is offered by Hegelian dialectics: far from being a story of its progressive overcoming, dialectics is for Hegel a systematic notation of the failure of all such attempts ... In other words, Hegelian 'reconciliation' is not a 'panlogicist' sublation of all reality in the Concept but a final consent to the fact that the Concept itself is 'not all' (to use a Lacanian term). In this sense ... Hegel ... [is] ... the first post-Marxist: he opened up the field of a certain fissure subsequently 'sutured' by Marxism. (Žižek, 1989, p. 6)

Let us sum up the main thrust of this first part of the chapter. We began with the suggestion that Žižek insists on maintaining a critical distinction between ideology and non-ideology. Of course, the manner in which he does this is rather paradoxical. Žižek asks us to consider the possibility of holding a position that will enable the maintenance of a critical stance against and beyond the ideologies we encounter in the social field (to repeat: 'we must ... maintain the tension that keeps the critique of ideology alive'). Yet, the idea that we could occupy such a position (a 'place from which one can denounce ideology') is immediately thought to be 'impossible': that is, the position of the critic is rendered purely empty, radically negative and irreducible to any 'positively determined reality'.

This, for Žižek, does not mean that the idea of actually engaging in ideology critique is lost to a negative abstraction. For we must, on this view, understand how 'radical negativity' also *necessarily* gives rise to a form of antagonism that structures our concrete experience of ideology. That is to say, the ideological and critical struggle over meaning in the symbolic realm (recall, for example, Birkin and Ursula's antagonistic exchange) is concretely structured in accordance with the 'Reality' that there is always something fundamentally lacking in any attempt to foreclose the social-ideological field. Every time a situated critic says 'No!' and challenges the harmony (say Birkin's notion of sexual harmony) or wholeness (say Stillman's idea of a world restored to the wholeness of God's word) projected in ideological symbolisations (s)he, for Žižek, unavoidably bears witness to the potentially disruptive power of the negative (see Žižek, 1989, pp. 230–231).

IDEOLOGY CRITIQUE AND THE AFFIRMATION OF ETHICS

Why, though, should any critic want to negate or challenge the harmony or wholeness projected in ideological symbolisations? This question is crucial in so far as it plunges us – we could say after a certain Habermasian fashion – into the murky waters of ethical motivation (see Habermas, 1987, p. 284). Žižek, as we shall see, provides a degree of clarity on this issue by consistently entrusting himself to the thought of Immanuel Kant. Put simply, Žižek's ideology critique is ethically motivated by concerns that are explicitly Kantian. Now, we can begin to detect this by considering a passage from his 'Beyond Discourse Analysis' (Žižek, 1990, pp. 249–260). Here Žižek explicitly raises the possibility of what he calls the 'ethics of the real'. We should say at this juncture that the essay in question is constituted as a formulated response and appraisal (an overwhelmingly positive one at that) of work undertaken by Ernesto Laclau and Chantal Mouffe in *Hegemony and Socialist Strategy*. Žižek writes:

> The main achievement of *Hegemony* ... is that, perhaps for the first time, it articulates the contours of a political project based on an ethics of the real, ... an ethics of confrontation with an impossible, traumatic kernel not covered by any ideal (of unbroken communication ...). That's why we can effectively say that *Hegemony* is the only real answer to Habermas, to his project based on the ethics of ... communication without constraint. The way Habermas formulates the 'ideal speech situation' already betrays its status as fetish: 'ideal speech situation' is something which, as soon as we engage in communication, is 'simultaneously denied and laid claim to', i.e. we must presuppose the ideal of an unbroken communication to be already realised, even

though we know simultaneously that this cannot be the case. (Žižek, 1990, p. 259)

We see that the 'ethics of the real', for Žižek, confronts us with the impossibility of regulating the communicative universe with reference to the 'ideal'. The implication, of course, is that ethics itself acquires the impossible status of what we have been calling the 'Real'. That is to say, it is the pure emptiness or 'radical negativity' (the 'traumatic kernel') pervading any supposedly transcendental regulative ideal – notice that Žižek explicitly targets Habermas's 'ideal speech situation' – that necessarily gives ethics a confrontational or, what we earlier called, antagonistic character. Now, although Žižek seems intent on criticising the notion of an 'ideal speech situation', he nonetheless formulates his 'ethics of the real' as 'the only real answer to Habermas'. This infers, of course, that Žižek thinks Habermas is at least asking pertinent and important ethical questions.

Žižek is drawn to the Kantianism in Habermas: that is to say, he is attracted to Habermas's Kantian-inspired affirmation of universality (see Habermas, 1990, p. 197). We can look to Žižek's critique of what he calls the 'ideology of late capitalism' for clear evidence of a similar universalist conviction. He asks the following ethical question:

> Where ... are we to look for the way out of [the] vicious circle of late-capitalis[m]? ... The way to break out of this vicious circle is ... to invent forms of political practice that contain a dimension of universality beyond Capital ... (Žižek, 1993, pp. 219–220)

So, according to Žižek, an ethically motivated critique of the 'vicious' ideology of late capitalism points to a 'dimension of universality beyond'. Again it is important to stress how this concept of the 'universal beyond' is 'Real' in Žižek's strict Lacanian use of the term. In other words, the universal – as 'Real' – has the paradoxical status of being both necessary and impossible. As ethically motivated critics of ideology we are, Žižek says after the Kantian fashion, necessarily and unavoidably involved in the symbolic activity of positing universals. Yet, the notion of positing a 'universal beyond' ideology is, on this view, something we perpetually encounter as an impossibility: that is, we inevitably experience the lack or incompleteness which pervades our specific ideological symbolisation of it. Žižek is again drawing inspiration from the work of Laclau. Consider the following passage from Žižek's *The Abyss of Freedom*:

> As Ernesto Laclau would ... put it, the Universal is simultaneously necessary (unavoidable) and impossible; necessary since ... the symbolic medium as such is universal, and impossible, since the positive content of the Universal is never purely neutral but is always (mis)appropriated, elevated from some particular content that 'hegemonises' the Universal ... (Žižek, 1997a, p. 53)

The 'ontological scandal', as Žižek would call it, of the universal – that is, the fact universality is impossible, always (mis)appropriated, etc. – acquires its sense in the performative enunciations of the 'subject' of ethical experience. What defines this ethical subject is its excessiveness (Žižek, 1999, pp. 291–292). The subject is *excessive* inasmuch as it has the performative power to construct or, we should say, *reconstruct* the ontological frameworks that positively sustain current forms of ethical life. Or, to put it another way: the subject, through its performative assumption of 'universal norms', constitutes a 'crack in the ontological edifice of the universe' (Žižek, 1997b, p. 214). Now, what makes this performative gesture understandable from an ethical point of view is, Žižek says, the fact that it implicates the subject in a field of moral responsibility. That is to say, the performative assumption of universal norms – the symbolic gesture of saying 'universal morality is X!' – simultaneously precipitates an assumption of moral responsibility on the part of the subject positing these norms. Again it is important to recognise that Žižek theorises this process in terms that he considers strictly Kantian. He writes:

> [T]he unique strength of Kant's ethics lies in ... [its] formal indeterminacy: moral Law does not tell me *what* my duty is, it merely tells me *that* I should accomplish my duty. That is to say, it is not possible to derive the concrete norms I have to follow in my specific situation from the moral Law itself – *which means that the subject himself has to assume the responsibility of translating the abstract injunction of the moral Law into a series of concrete obligations*. In this precise sense, ... the ethical subject bears full responsibility for the concrete universal norms he follows – that is to say, the only guarantor of the universality of positive moral norms is the subject's own contingent act of performatively assuming these norms. (Žižek, 1997b, p. 214)

So we see that Kantian 'moral Law', for Žižek, amounts to an ethical injunction – to do one's duty – that must always be responsibly translated into a 'series of concrete obligations'. Let us, once again, return to Stillman in order to animate this idea. Stillman, on Žižek's Kantian terms, fails in his duty to act morally in so far as he exhibits no responsibility for the normative standpoint he adopts. That is to say, Stillman, in his normative pursuit of God's language, labours under a promise of ethical transcendence that is taken to instrumentally override or displace any responsible consideration of the pain he is causing the other (namely, his son). Or, consider the situation of an alleged 'sex addict' who is caught by a spouse in the throes of sexual – and extra-marital – congress. The 'sex addict' could try to displace, or instrumentally override, any responsible obligation to the other (in this case, the spouse) by suggesting that he is suffering at the hands of a biological affliction over which no control can be exercised. In this case, of course, the notion of a 'biological affliction' is ideologically posited to assume the responsibilities and obligations the subject ('sex addict') displaces.

Žižekian critique is of ethical importance in so far as it rejects such an ideological displacement of moral responsibility (see Žižek, 1993, pp. 99–100). But what, we may ask, if the subject can be said to act responsibly, dutifully and yet *unethically*? This question brings into focus what is perhaps the fundamental difficulty facing any affirmation of Kantian 'moral Law': that is to say, it forces us to confront the potentially monstrous or evil consequences that may flow from consistently following it through. The terroristic ethic of the 'suicide bomber' would seem to present an exemplary case of a subject consistently following a course of action dictated in accordance with 'moral Law'. To put it in the form of a question: are not the actions of the terrorist formally dutiful and responsible in Žižek's strict Kantian sense (performing a duty for the sake of an ethno-religious cause, responsibly exhibiting a will to do God's work or good no matter the cost to the self, etc.)? Is this not an example of what Žižek, again following Kant, calls 'diabolical Evil'; the 'act of elevating Evil into an ethical principle'? (Žižek, 1993, p. 101).

In order to rescue his Kantian-inspired ethic of responsibility, Žižek must critically expose the concrete expression or symbolisation of 'diabolical Evil' as ideological self-deception (see Žižek, 1997b, p. 231). The 'suicide bomber', in this regard, must be viewed as someone so instrumentally swept up in a form of the 'Good' that (s)he fails to recognise or displaces the horrifyingly monstrous consequences of her/his actions. Žižek, we can see, adopts this strategy in a discussion of the 'Nazi executioners' of the Holocaust. He is keen to defend the Kantian ethic of responsibility against the criticism – detectable, he says, in the work of Hannah Arendt amongst others – that the ethos of Nazism was systematically over-coded with the formalist Kantian attitude to do one's duty for the sake of duty. Žižek's point is that Nazism (and by implication the activities of the 'suicide bomber' mentioned above), far from exhibiting a formalist attitude, actually:

> violated the basic Kantian precept of the primacy of Duty over any notion of Good, since it relied on a precise notion of Good (the establishment of a true community of German people) ... to which all 'formal' ethical injunctions were instrumentalised and relativised (it is proper to kill, torture ... if it serves the higher goal of the German community). The element which suspended the 'formalist' character of Nazi normativity was the very reference to the Führer: ... the Führer is the one who *knows what is for the Good of the People* and, consequently, [his] word overrides all 'formalist' ethical considerations. (Žižek, 1997b, p. 231)

In this regard, Žižekian ethics asserts the 'formalist' primacy of Duty over and above any substantive form of the 'Good' (fundamentalism, Nazism, etc.) that may want to step into the breach of the social-ideological field. This, of course, is where responsibility ought to be brought into the equation. To repeat: it is in the subject's translation of the abstract injunction – to do one's duty – that (s)he assumes responsibility for the goods that structure ethical life. In a sense, then, Žižek's ethically motivated critique of ideology is defined by the way in which it can formally problematise the goods that are taken to legitimise morally irresponsible action.

It is important to stress that the position from which this critique originates is – in Žižek's Lacanian and *Realist* terms – impossible to occupy and yet necessarily unavoidable. In other words, the 'moral act' of assuming responsibility for the 'Good' is *impossible*, according to Žižekian logic, in that we can never be absolutely certain as to whether or not our duty to this 'Good' is instrumentally or pathologically driven. Consequently, the rather precarious circumstances in which we exercise our duty act as a *necessary* limit that cannot simply be avoided or, as Žižek says, 'transgressed' in a 'pure act of reason'. In sum: Žižek's affirmation of moral responsibility and 'Duty' must give way to the powerful negativity or, in this context, 'formalism' of the 'Real' qua impossible/unavoidable ethical injunction (Žižek, 1997b, p. 231).

We began this second part by raising the question of what ethically motivates ideology critique. Žižek, we saw, gives Kantian-inspired responses to this question. Most immediately, we saw the extent to which Žižek affirms the Kantian conviction that ethical criticism must be motivated by 'universal' concerns. That is to say, the notion of critique points to a 'universality beyond' the ideologies currently structuring ethical life. Characteristically, Žižek gives this notion of 'universality' a Lacanian twist; thus the universal – qua 'Real' – acquires the paradoxical status of being both necessary and impossible. To repeat: as ethically motivated critics of ideology, we are necessarily involved in the symbolic activity of positing universals. Yet, the notion of positing a 'universal beyond' ideology is something we perpetually encounter as impossible: that is, we inevitably experience the lack or incompleteness that pervades our ideological symbolisation of it. In this sense, of course, the ethically motivated critic is, for Žižek, always left in the precarious position of contemplating the possibility of her/his own specific failure to move beyond ideology.

Now, it would be clearly wrong to say that this conclusion forces Žižek into a nihilistic dismissal of ethical matters. For there is a sense in which our specific failure – to constitute a universal norm beyond ideology – gives rise to the possibility of affirming a form of Kantian moral responsibility. To repeat: the performative affirmation of universal norms – the particular and failed symbolic gesture of saying 'the moral Law is X!' – simultaneously, for Žižek, precipitates the assumption of moral responsibility on the part of the subject positing these norms. This brings into focus the suggestion that Žižek wants, as we earlier put it, to implicate the subject (Stillman, the 'sex addict', etc.) in a field of moral responsibility. Also, it brings into focus the extent to which Žižek's ethically motivated critique is defined by the way it seeks to question the ideological displacement of obligations and responsibilities.

CONCLUSION

Nothing we have said so far has explicitly focused on the consistency of Žižek's views. Yet, everything we have said points to inevitable questions concerning the way in which the two strains of his thought mapped out above (negative and affirmative) are related to one another. It will be the aim of our conclusion to think through the way in which Žižek theoretically relates these tendencies and briefly to make some critical remarks about the consistency he lends to them. Also, we shall briefly consider how these strains of Žižekian thought may help us evaluate the notion that we can experience a world beyond ideology.

Let us begin, then, by briefly clarifying the negative and affirmative strains in Žižek's thought as articulated. Firstly, let us think about how Žižek relates the idea of negativity to ideology critique. We have seen (in the first part of the chapter) the way in which Žižek uses the negative as a conceptual tool in his critical stand against ideology. That is to say, we have seen the way in which he insists on theorising the position of the critic (the 'place from which one can denounce ideology') negatively, and how this negativity is thought to fuel challenges against the foreclosure of social-ideological field (think again of the exchanges between Gerald and Birkin, Birkin and Ursula, etc.). To repeat: ideological struggle or antagonistic critique always and concretely bears witness to the disruptive power of the negative. Put all too simply, saying 'No!' to the harmony or wholeness projected in ideological symbolisations is, according to Žižekian logic, what critics of ideology do.

Yet, conversely, the Žižekian critic of ideology is also (as we saw in the second part of the chapter) engaged in an ethical 'Yes' saying. That is to say, Žižek responds affirmatively to the question of why be ethically motivated to engage in ideology critique by positively championing Kantian notions of universality and moral responsibility. To repeat: the critic of ideology, from a Žižekian perspective, must accept responsibility for the 'universal norms' (s)he posits in the social field. (S)he must retain an awareness of how ideology can function to excuse or justify morally irresponsible actions (our 'sex addict' again comes to mind). Also, and perhaps most importantly, (s)he must be critically sensitive to the fact that her/his own ethical position in the symbolic realm is morally precarious: that is, surrounded by uncertainty.

Such are the negative and affirmative strains of Žižek's thinking. Let us now briefly venture some critical remarks concerning the consistency that is lent to them. Or, consider the following question: does the affirmative and ethical strain in Žižek's thinking always already render his stress on negativity rather redundant? The implication of this question is that Žižek's notion of ideology critique only makes sense if it is normatively grounded in a Kantian ethic that has nothing really do with the so-called 'pure' or 'radical' 'negativity' of the 'Real'. On this view, the position of the critic is never 'empty' or 'impossible', but is always affirmatively concerned with 'moral responsibility', actively justifying 'universal norms', etc. To put it in the form of another question: how can an ethically motivated critique such as Žižek's be anything other than a positive transgression of an impossible or radically negative 'Real'?

Žižek is well aware of this potential criticism and aims to challenge it head on. Indeed, this is already implied in his spirited defence of the 'moral Law' above. Rather than concede that the ethical motivation to critique and transform the social-ideological field be thought of as a transgression of negativity (a Nazi transgression, a fundamentalist transgression, etc.), Žižek, to repeat, insists on its 'formal indeterminacy'. Žižek's point, here, is that the 'radical negativity' of the 'Real' – understood in this context as the 'formal indeterminacy' of 'Duty' – *unavoidably and immediately persists in the subject's motivation to assume moral responsibility*. That is to say, the subject cannot simply avoid the ethical injunction to act in accordance with 'Duty'. So, for Žižek, it is not that we positively transgress the 'radical negativity', 'impossibility', 'Reality' or 'formalism' of 'Duty': rather, we immediately experience it as the constitutive uncertainty surrounding the assumption of 'moral responsibility' in the symbolic realm. Negativity, in this sense, is not a redundant abstraction existing beyond our experiences in the symbolic, but is *absolutely immanent* to the limited and precarious task of affirming an ethical standpoint in the social field (see, Žižek, 1997b, p. 217).

We are perhaps now in a better position to evaluate the precise terms in which Žižek theoretically relates the affirmative and negative strains of his thought. Negativity assumes sovereignty and is given conceptual priority over affirmation. To repeat: it is the 'radical negativity' of the 'Real' – the 'formal indeterminacy' of 'Duty' – that provides the condition of possibility for affirming an ethical standpoint in the symbolic realm. To repeat an even earlier point: it is the 'radical negativity' of the 'Real' – its 'impossibility', pure emptiness, etc. – that allows us to positively and antagonistic-ally struggle over the ideological meanings of subject-positions adopted in the social field. To the critical suggestion that all this emphasis on negativity inevitably leads to abstraction, Žižek, we have seen, insists that it is a 'necessary' feature of social life: that is to say, the conceptual priority given to negativity is never, on this view, a purely theoretical matter, but is always taken to be constitutive of the subject's concrete experience of ideology.

Let us now close our discussion by considering how these strains in Žižek's thinking may help us evaluate the notion that we can experience a world beyond ideology. Well, if a critical stand against ideology is, as Žižek says, motivated by a positive commitment to a form of Kantian universalism and moral responsibility, and if these ethical characteristics are formally and immanently haunted by the spectre of 'radical negativity', then the problem of experiencing a world beyond ideology is a *paradoxical* one. In other words, the 'stepping out' of ideology – positively inhabiting a moral universe in which we are certain in our exercise of 'Duty', 'moral responsibility' etc. – always already involves our potential 'enslavement' to a form of the 'Good' that may ideologically repress certain subjects in the social field. *So, to the prospect of concretely experiencing a world beyond ideology Žižek gives a categorical 'Yes!' and 'No!'* Yes, we can take a stand against ideology. No, we can never be certain of the terms of our own ideological enslavement. Yes, we can maintain a critical position enabling us to point up and negate the limits of ideologies we encounter in the social field. No, we can never inhabit a social field totally purged of ideology.

Of course, it would be easy to critically dismiss Žižek's logic as paradoxical and contradictory, to suggest that his philosophical shilly-shallying is of little practical meaning or significance. But this would miss the crucial point of the Žižekian enterprise: for we have seen how Žižek embraces this paradoxical logic and how he theoretically puts it to work in his analysis of our concrete experience of ideology. Further, he would say that the making of such criticisms serves as an immediate reminder of the real and practical struggle over meaning that exists in the symbolic realm. The experience of such 'antagonism', on Žižek's view, signifies not only the continual work of ideology, but also our continuing ethical desire to move beyond it.

REFERENCES

Auster, P. (1992) *The New York Trilogy* (London: Faber and Faber).
Deleuze, G. (1986) *Nietzsche and Philosophy* (London: Athlone).
Habermas, J. (1987) *The Philosophical Discourse of Modernity* (Cambridge: Polity Press).
Habermas, J. (1990) *Moral Consciousness and Communicative Action* (Cambridge: Polity Press).
Lawrence, D. H. (1996) *Women In Love* (London: Penguin).

Žižek, S. (1989) *The Sublime Object of Ideology* (London: Verso).
Žižek, S. (1990) 'Beyond Discourse Analysis', in E. Laclau, *New Reflections on the Revolution of Our Time* (London: Verso).
Žižek, S. (1993) *Tarrying with the Negative: Kant, Hegel and the Critique of Ideology* (Durham: Duke University Press).
Žižek, S. (ed.) (1994) *Mapping Ideology* (London: Verso).
Žižek, S. (1997a) *The Abyss of Freedom* (Michigan: University of Michigan Press).
Žižek, S. (1997b) *The Plague of Fantasies* (London: Verso).
Žižek, S. (1999) *The Žižek Reader* eds E. & E. Wright (Oxford: Blackwell).

4 City Life and the Conditions of Possibility of an Ideology-Proof Subject: Simmel, Benjamin and Joyce on Berlin, Paris and Dublin

Kieran Keohane

Simmel, Benjamin and Joyce are the three figures of classical modernism with the strongest affinity to postmodernism. Indeed in their respective fields of sociology, cultural criticism and literature, they are frequently discussed as though they were 'postmodernists before their time', presaging and exemplifying the theoretical, methodological, and aesthetic sensibilities that have lately come together under the umbrella of postmodernism. Underappreciated at the time, it is as if they have now come into their own as, if not 'founding fathers' then certainly 'forefathers' of the present generation. If we are to understand the status of ideology in the context of the conditions of postmodernity, and develop tactics of ideology critique appropriate to these conditions, then it will be instructive for us to look at how these three writers have dealt with the problem.

Simmel, Benjamin and Joyce, writing of Berlin, Paris and Dublin respectively, cities that they simultaneously loved and hated, feared and celebrated, are acutely aware of the problems of modern urban life, but are also attuned to its joys and alive to its utopian possibilities. They have in common the conviction that while the modern city has many ominous dimensions – predatory commercialism, social conflict grounded in inequalities of class and ethnicity, deprivation and marginalisation, the reduction of value to cash and the debasement of the human spirit – the city also constitutes the conditions of possibility of realising the good life in modern society. For Simmel, Benjamin and Joyce, the city is the locus of modernity, and its symbolic order and imaginative structure are characterised by ambiguity and ambivalence. On the one hand the city threatens the erasure of individuality by the mass, and simultaneously the city provides the anonymity and freedom for subjective self-expression and the celebration of individuality. The city constitutes a theatre of power and ideology, of collective action and difference of opinion – a *polis* – and cultivates its subjective correspondent(s); the person who is subject to ideology, and simultaneously the open-minded, liberal democratic, individual citizen.

As Simmel expresses it:

> The deepest problems of modern life spring from the attempt of the individual to maintain the independence and individuality of his existence against the sovereign powers of society, against the weight of historical heritage and the external culture and technique of life. (Simmel, 1971, p. 325)

This dialectic between objective and subjective culture, between the homogenising effects of mass society and the fragmentation of collective life into privatised individualism, the problem of finding the good relation between our individual and our social being – a problem of the care of the self – animates the writings of Simmel, Benjamin and Joyce, and is still at the core of discourse on the city at the turn of the twenty-first century.

For Simmel, Benjamin and Joyce, as we are both subjects and objects of modernity, the subject of ideology is also, equally, the subject who is resilient to ideology. The metropolis constitutes a form of life in which the individual is subject to the sovereign powers of society, but simultaneously a form which generates the conditions of possibility for the emergence of a modern 'ideal type' of subject resilient to power. For Simmel this is the 'blasé cosmopolitan', a subject who is intellectualistic, liberal, tolerant of difference, and who thrives on the agonal pluralism of urban life (Simmel, 1971). For Walter Benjamin the equivalent is the *flâneur*, a participant observer in urban phantasmagoria, but one who cultivates distance from the prevailing ideologies, enabling a critical perspective and preserving the possibility of an alternative form of life;[1] and the qualities of the blasé cosmopolitan and the *flâneur* are personified in Joyce's character Leopold Bloom, the hero of *Ulysses* (Joyce, 1990).

Dublin, Berlin and Paris, cities with very different modern histories: Paris the capital city of an empire, a global power, capital of the nineteenth century; Berlin, capital of Prussia, a regional power underpinned by a Spartan militaristic and bureaucratic culture with national and imperial aspirations; Dublin, in the same time-frame, a subjected city, the subaltern capital of Britain's oldest and most troublesome colony. Monet and Renoir depicted Paris as the city of light and life; Joyce represented Dublin in paralysis, darkness and death. And today, at the turn of the twenty-first century, Paris has become like Rome, which, as Joyce remarked, is like someone who makes his living by charging money to see his grandmother's corpse (Ellmann, 1982, p. 225). Paris is the world's largest single tourist destination, where people pay to see the remains of classical nineteenth-century modernity. Berlin, the forgotten city, walled and divided, the forbidden city, twice thwarted in its designs to be capital of Europe, capital of the twentieth century, is poised at last to become capital of Germany and the European Union. And 'dear old dirty Dublin', Europe's worst slum in 1900, the squalid, backward capital of Europe's third-world country throughout the twentieth century, is a brash, bustling, trendy city that boasts itself 'the new Paris'!

But despite the evident differences between Paris, Berlin and Dublin, what collects them, what allows us to move freely from discussing one to the other? Georg Simmel argues that what modern cities share in common are the conditions that cultivate a unique form of modern subjectivity (Simmel, 1971).[2] The collective and subjective existential conditions that characterise the modern metropolitan form of life, Simmel argues, are that in the metropolis there arises 'an intensification of emotional life due to the swift and continuous shift of external and internal stimuli' (1971, p. 325). In the metropolis there is an exponential growth and expansion of possibilities for encounters with alterity, arising from the dense overlapping and interpenetration of elements. Thus, 'the relationships and concerns of the typical metropolitan resident are so manifold and complex ... as a result of the agglomeration of so many persons with such differentiated interests, their relationships and activities intertwine with one another into a many membered organism' (1971, p. 328). These conditions become ramified into thousands of individual variations, bearing the characteristic stamp of each particular city. But while the *content* of life in every modern environment will be irreducibly particular, giving every place its unique and peculiar character, there is a generalised, ubiquitous *form* in modern urban life the world over. Berliners, Parisians and Dubliners (and New Yorkers, for that matter) as urbanites share a common form of life.

Simmel lived in downtown Berlin, at the intersection of Leipziger-strasse and Friedrichstrasse, the subway stop on his doorstep was Stadmitte (mid-town), in an area that was the heart of Berlin before it was obliterated in the Second World War, left a wasteland for 50 years, and is presently the world's largest building site. Potsdamer Platz and Checkpoint Charlie are a minute's walk north and south of his house. In the liveliness of this downtown environment Simmel formulates the archetypal modern subject that corresponds with the metropolis as the city dweller whose 'essentially intellectu-alistic character' distinguishes him from the mental life of the small town, which rests more on feelings and emotional relationships. The metropolitan person has become accustomed to jarring contrasts and rapid changes, movement and discontinuity, and in order to live in this vibrant modern environment: 'The Metropolitan type – which naturally takes on a thousand individual modifications – creates a protective organ for itself against the profound disruption with which the fluctuations and discontinuities of the external milieu threaten it' (Simmel, 1971, p. 326). Simmel says that 'with every crossing of the street, with the tempo and multiplicity of economic, occupational and social life' (Simmel, 1971, p. 325), the metropolis creates the sensory foundations on which a new subjectivity is con-structed. Echoing Simmel, in a typical passage of *Ulysses*, as Bloom walks along Talbot street at the edge of Dublin's red-light district, he crosses the street to avoid a lurching drunk, he is narrowly missed by two cyclists, he is nearly run over by a street-car, he has two kids bump into him (causing him to check his pockets, as he suspects it is a pickpocket's ruse), he skirts a rowdy gang outside a pub, he is hailed by three prostitutes and an old bawd pimping a teenager, and he bumps into (or imagines what he would say if he were to bump into) a respectable acquaintance and has to account for his being in the red-light district to her; all in a 50-yard walk (Joyce, 1990, pp. 410–418). The new subjectivity of the metropolitan is acutely aware and self-aware, calculating and self-reflexive. He is self-possessed, and at the same time immersed in the crowd, subject to the sovereign powers of mass society and at the same time resilient and skilled in evading interpellation.

The second formative influence on modern mental life, Simmel says, is the universalisation of the money economy, which becomes 'a common denominator of all values ... the frightful leveller that hollows out the core of things, their peculiarities, their specific values and their uniqueness and incomparability ... all float with the same specific gravity in the constantly moving stream of money' (Simmel, 1971, pp. 329–330). These two influences combine, Simmel argues, to cultivate a psychic phenomenon that uniquely characterises the modern metropolitan subject, that is 'the blasé outlook'.

> The essence of the blasé attitude is an indifference to the distinctions between things. Not in the sense that they are not perceived, ... but rather that the meaning and the value of the distinctions between things, and therewith of the things themselves, are experienced as meaningless. They appear to the blasé person in a homogenous, flat and grey colour with no one of them worthy of being preferred to another. (Simmel, 1971, p. 330)

Other aspects of the blasé outlook which Simmel discerns are 'reserve', the 'privilege of suspicion', 'a slight aversion, a mutual strangeness and repulsion', 'antipathy ... which brings about the sort of distanciation and deflection without which this kind of life could not be carried on at all' (Simmel, 1971, p. 331).

But the crucial point for Simmel is that he sees how these qualities, which at first sight might be seen to be solely negative attributes of modern subjectivity, are also, paradoxically, the very grounds of modern tolerance, liberalism and cosmopolitanism. The blasé attitude is a new 'protective organ', developed to protect the personality (Simmel, 1971, p. 326). For Simmel the cosmopolitan is not inhumane, but on the contrary, is more fully human. The citizen with the blasé attitude is used to difference and discontinuity, he is accustomed to the antagonism of modern life. Ordinarily he is able to deal with it. At worst he is indifferent to it, or at least he can tolerate it. At best he is friendly towards it, he feels at home in the middle of it, and actively seeks it out. Prevailing ideological currents do not easily sway the blasé cosmopolitan. When he is hailed (interpellated) he may not respond: he has heard it all before. He is not naively subject to sentimental and emotional appeals: he 'enjoys the privilege of suspicion' (Simmel, 1971, p. 331). Rational and calculating, he is inclined to size up the situation objectively and (he likes to imagine) make up his own mind – as much as possible, under the circumstances! He is self-reflexive and ironic even on the subject of his own autonomy.

For Simmel this is the deeply ambiguous effect of the combination of increasing rationalisation and the complete penetration of the money economy: on the one hand it frees Berliners from localism and chauvinism, but on the other hand it leaves them open to instrumental and strategic rationality. The ambiguous effect of the rationalised consciousness of urban life that is the subjective correlate of the intensification of nervous stimulation and the abstraction of the money economy is that it frees urbanites from servitude to ideology, chauvinism, and prejudice; but, simultaneously, as the universal solvent, money is 'the frightful leveller – it hollows out the core of things' (Simmel, 1971, p. 330), making social relations inhumane. The rationalisation of consciousness which accompanies the universalisation of the money economy might free Berliners from anti-Semitism, but it might also provide the foundations for a new barbarism of reason, which, alloyed with the mutual antipathy characteristic of life amongst strangers, and the vestiges of traditional prejudice and military authoritarianism, was to become the basis for the Holocaust.

Walter Benjamin similarly sees an ambiguous quality in the city's ideological currents. The city is a phantasmagoria of the ideology of progress, and the fundamental component of the phantasmagoria is the commodity fetish (Benjamin, 1995, p. 50). Progress is worshipped by the consumption of commodities and fashion 'prescribes the ritual by which Progress wishes to be worshipped' (Benjamin, 1995). But this phantasmagoria generates a material and symbolic leftover, an excess of 'dialectical images' – 'small particular moments' in which the 'total historical event' could be discovered (Buck-Morss, 1995, p. 71). These moments, like Joycean 'epiphanies', can illuminate the social totality for the subject who encounters them and brush against the grain of the phantasmagoria of progress. Modern cities are littered with the ruins of progress: once-fashionable shops and districts, presently dilapidated; outmoded commodities discarded as detritus; a negative excess piling up in a repressed collective unconscious of consumer society, returning and protruding into the dream world of the present. To Benjamin, the Paris Arcades, the prototypical shopping malls and supermarkets, now defunct, and lying like petrified forests of consumer enjoyment[3] were such ruins, a stone's throw from Galeries Lafayette and Le Printemps. Formerly 'grottoes of the commodity fetish' (Benjamin, 1995), they persisted in Benjamin's time as nightmarish passages to the underworld, peopled with the mouldering cadavers of mannequins; awkwardly poised, grotesquely dismembered and contorted, draped in ludicrous costumes and festooned in cobwebs and grime, they represented the *ur*-phenomena of the Real, stark reminders of the constitutive lack in the commodity fetish (Buck-Morss, 1995, pp. 56–75). What had once been the 'sublime objects of ideology' (Žižek, 1989) now appear as profane and ridiculous. Benjamin argues that the dialectical image of the outmoded commodity, in which the lack that had once been the focus of desire where consumer fantasies were projected and elaborated, and thus the source of the sex-appeal of the commodity fetish, now appears as gaping void, may strike at the heart of the belief in progress and the entire mythology. To the day-dream believer in progress, believing in the eternity of the forever-renewed present-as-future life everlasting, encounter with such dialectical images would be the modern/secular equivalent of encounter with the mark of the Anti-Christ.

But the grottoes of the commodity fetish, petrified and obsolete in Benjamin's time, are revivified, and are being revivified now, and new (olde) passages are being built. '*Les Passages couverts*' are featured in the centre pages of *Paris: Môde d'emploi 1999*, the official guide to Paris produced by the *Office de Tourisme et des Congrès Paris*, and distributed free to hotels, airports, and travel agents around the world.

In Dublin the equivalent of the decayed Paris Arcades used to be Temple Bar;[4] once a thriving network of streets, but more recently a ruin, a run-down district of derelict shops and seedy bars at the heart of Dublin. In the 1990s Temple Bar was targeted for redevelopment, and over five years some £300 million has been spent to turn the area into the capital's cultural district,[5] 'Dublin's Left Bank', and Dublin is hyped by the tourism industry as 'the new Paris'. And in Berlin what had been the city centre for the first half of the twentieth century was waste land and no man's land for the next 50 years, a monument to the frozen ideological polarities of modernity, but in the last decade it has become a building site of epic proportions, a tourist spectacle in its own right. The Paris Passages, Berlin's Potsdamer Platz and Dublin's Temple Bar now trade in signs of the renaissance of modernity. In the postmodern, nostalgic imaginary they become vistas and passageways not to the hellish underworld of dead and decaying modernity, but to classical modernity as a wholesome past, or more precisely, to simulacra of classical modern urbanism as a form of life in such a past.

The Puces de St Ouen, the Paris Flea Market, used to sell off the detritus of the nobility to the peasantry at the edge of the city. Now a new passage, resembling Benjamin's Passages downtown, has been cut through the flea market, and accommodates a different class of customer:

> In the heart of St Ouen Flea Market, the *Marché Dauphine*: Come and discover 150 antique shops on two floors in the *Marché Dauphine*. You will find paintings, furniture, ornaments and curiosities of all periods. The *Marché Dauphine* offers a unique service: issuing certificates of authenticity to buyers established by independent experts ... (Marché Dauphine publicity leaflet, 1999)

The Marché Dauphine sells the detritus of the modern bourgeoisie to their inheritors, postmodern homemakers in search of the authentic. As well as nineteenth- and twentieth-century furniture, paintings and ornaments, and new-wave primitivism and orientalism (shops are dedicated to Africa, Indian exotic artefacts, Judaica, Moroccan tribal rugs, etc.), Marché Dauphine has boutiques that specialise in 'vintage' advertising posters and 'classic' publicity objects from theatre and cinema, 'antique' cameras, toys, household appliances, comics, records, luggage, clothes and costumes. In the Marché Dauphine a schoolroom map of the Empire circa 1910, with the caption 'les Francais: C'est ici, votre Empire' costs 2,000 Fr. *Tintin en Congo*, a comic book from the 1940s, recently sold for 100,000 Fr at a Paris auction ('Six Minutes News Bulletin', Paris TV Channel 6, 28 November 1998). As Benjamin says, on the totemic tree of objects within the primal thicket, the very last face on the totem is that of kitsch.

But Benjamin didn't fully anticipate the speed at which 'antique' can constitute a second life of the mass-market commodity, after it has been shorn of its value. And in the accelerated culture of late modernity and the exhaustion of cultural innovation of postmodernity, the time/space between the devalued category of 'refuse', on the one hand, and the revalued categories of 'old-fashioned', 'retro', 'classic', 'vintage' and 'antique' on the other, become windows of opportunity where outmoded commodities can be re-presented with new representational values. The subversive potential of the outmoded commodity as dialectical image is erased when the outmoded commodity is resurrected from the dead and re-presented for consumption as 'vintage' or 'antique', revivified and reinvigorated with renewed fetish qualities. Perhaps even more than previously, for in its new life as an antique its representational value is history, time. It is placed outside/above the risk of temporal flux, it transcends the diachronic forces that give fashion its anxiety; antique is a quality that never goes out of style. By its miraculous survival from the flux of history it serves as a quilting point that reassures and reconfirms the value of the commodity. In becoming antique the outmoded commodity partakes of a cunning of logic by which the destructive forces of Time in fact are not destructive to the Utopian, dreamy investment in futurity, but actually have redemptive power.

In the time-frame of Joyce's *Ulysses*, Dublin city centre, around Temple Bar, was alive with social antagonism, arising from all classes and manner of people living cheek by jowl and on top of one another. Tenements and town houses stood back to back and facing onto one another. Trinity College's young gentlemen, Guinness' brewery working men, squaddies from the garrison and shopkeepers, all rubbing shoulders and fighting for elbow room along the less than a mile of city streets between Trinity College and Guinness' brewery, Dublin Castle and the street markets. By the late nineteenth century Dublin was widely acknowledged to be the most over-crowded city and to have the worst slums in Europe. This teeming cauldron was dangerously charged with crime and sedition, and as the garrison expanded so the brothels and prostitutes did a roaring trade. Dublin's 'Monto' (Nighttown in Joyce's *Ulysses*) had more prostitutes per head than any other European city, and Dublin was to the British army in the 1890s what Saigon was to American troops in the 1960s. This was the context of friction, of random encounter, of vibrant social antagonism, on the streets, in the markets, in the brothels and especially in the pubs, in which the sensibility and the idiom of the modern Irish urban character was forged, and it is the forging of this character that Joyce reveals for us in the young Stephen and the mature Bloom (both aspects of himself and Everyman) in the epic of the modern Ulysses.

And this immediate juxtapositioning of social difference is still evident in the present, reconstructed simulacrum of Temple Bar – though it is in imminent danger of erasure. The Dublin Workingman's Club adjoins the £1,000 a-night Clarence Hotel, restored to its art deco glory by owners U2 (the club has recently been bought, and closed for redevelopment) and the James Connolly bookstore, named after labour leader and founder of the Citizens' Army as the vanguard of the working class, nestles amongst the cappuccino bars, terraces, and 'art spaces'. The 're-enchantment of Temple Bar' (Corcoran, 1998) has been good for business at James

Connolly's: tourists and Dubliners snaffle up Heaney and Joyce, histories of the Famine and 1798, while Marx has been shifted to the back of the store, and lapel pins of Lenin sell as novelty items at the cash desk. Consumers want interpretations of history – with the representational value of authenticity: 'I got it in Dublin actually, in Connolly's.' 'Really! Looks interesting. Must read it sometime' – but they have little interest in changing it! What still makes Temple Bar an interesting and vestigially modern city space is that the visitor might enjoy a *latte* while reading the *New York Times* or *La Monde*, and immediately outside the door have to give a junkie a wide berth – Dublin's heroin addicts have found easy pickings amongst the yuppies and tourists, particularly young people on English language and literary summer schools. In the middle of Temple Bar's £250k apartment zone is Focuspoint drop-in centre for the homeless, where a coffee is one-tenth what it costs next door, and where Dublin's destitute and Romanian Gypsy refugee claimants come to hang out. And at night, neo-urbanites who have bought a pad in Temple Bar on the promise/expectation of a 'sophisticated downtown lifestyle' have to pick their way through 'stag-ers' and 'hen-ers' on weekend package pub crawls from Liverpool and London, throwing up and falling down outside the 'olde' (or rather, 'auld') and 'unique' pubs and clubs. But even this form of life, which offered at least some possibilities for encounters with alterity, has recently been expunged from the urban scene, as the development corporation, Temple Bar Properties Ltd, has required that publicans no longer cater for such parties.

What once made the Paris Passages, Berlin's Potsdamer Platz and Dublin's Temple Bar modern urban spaces was the opportunity they provided for dialectical encounters between subjective and objective culture, between the citizen and the prevailing ideological powers: the magnificence of Empire, the heroic solidarity of Nation, the holy faith of our fathers, the truth of science, the phantasmagoria of progress; and simultaneously for encounters that provided opportunities for alternative perspectives: for Simmel, immersion in the multitude and the abstraction of money enabled detachment and intellectualism; for Benjamin, encounters with dialectical images – fragments, ruins, the ideological detritus of former hegemonies – that as profane (ridiculous) objects of ideology give the lie to the present regime's claim to permanence. Along the boulevards of Paris and Berlin, and in the passages and shops particularly, the *flâneur* and the blasé cosmopolitan were formed by reflexive encounters with power and ideology: the infinity of the Empire's magnificence, the enormity of the monuments like the Arc de Triomphe, the *grands places* and the impressive aspect of the public architecture, deliberately intended to dwarf and disempower the subject. By the mid-nineteenth century this was already an archaic and vestigial form of power. The emergent form assailed the modern subject in the Passages, in the Galeries Lafayette, and in the Opera, and it took the form of a relentless interpellation to consume. More particularly the growth of objective culture, the desiring machines of the emerging consumer society, confronted and exposed the *flâneur* to the infinity of his own desire: aggressively and systematically assailed by the new machines of advertising, marketing and publicity, he was interpellated that his every desire be met: all fantasies, whims, curiosities, needs and wants – real, imagined, and not yet even dreamt of – '... gastronomical perfections, intoxicating drinks, wealth without labour at the roulette wheel, gaiety in the vaudeville theatres, and in the first floor galleries, transports of sexual pleasure sold by a heavenly host of fashionably dressed ladies of the night' (Buck-Morss, 1995, p. 83).

It is in this context wherein the individual subject becomes the focus of systematic and relentless interpellation that the question of the care of the self assumes its contemporary relevance and urgency. Foucault shows that for the Greeks 'not to be a slave (of another city, of those who surround you, of those who govern you, of one's own passions)' was vitally important (Foucault, 1990). Not to become a slave required a 'care of the self', that is, 'the deliberate practice of liberty'. Care of the self entails sustained self-reflection, a systematic effort 'to know oneself, and to improve oneself, to master the appetites that risk engulfing you'. The importance of the practice of the care of the self for the Greeks, and more importantly for the modern city dweller is that

> the one who cared for himself correctly found himself, by that very fact, in a measure to behave correctly in relationship to others and for others. A city in which everyone would be correctly concerned for self would be a city that would be doing well, and it would find therein the ethical principle of its stability. (Foucault, 1998, pp. 4–7)

It is their identification of conditions of possibility of such a practice of the care of the self, and their illumination of the forms of life, that exemplify the practice in the modern metropolis that collects the work of Simmel, Benjamin and Joyce.

To survive in the modern city the subject had to learn to resist, to detach himself, to defer and to select gratifications, to respond, as Simmel argues, intellectually rather than emotionally. 'Curiosities aroused, fantasies indulged' promises an old sign still hanging in the Passage des Panoramas. And in addition to this aggressive, systematic deployment of power in the Passages, and on Haussmann's new streets, hacked through old, poorer quarters, the *flâneur* ran into, brushed past, skirted around and was confronted and harangued by hucksters, dealers, destitutes, salesmen, muggers, shoppers, pimps, prostitutes, policemen; his betters and his inferiors, strangers all. This is the texture of modern urban life in Simmel's Berlin, Benjamin's Paris and Joyce's Dublin. The blasé cosmopolitan, the *flâneur*, made his life amongst these strangers, made an art of reading and inter-preting them, found his *jouissance* in the social antagonism, the *frisson* of being with them, and made an emancipatory ethical principle of his being exemplary to them as a form of life practising a care of the self; offering heroic resistance to interpellation by the prevailing ideologies to which they, and he too, were interminably subject.

Joyce set out 'to forge in the smithy of my soul the uncreated conscience of my race' (Joyce, 1987), a model, prototype modern subject with the highly tuned intellect and blasé cosmopolitan outlook and the involved detachment of the *flâneur*. These are qualities that would enable him to defend himself against the onslaught of ideological interpellation – imperial propaganda, reac-tionary chauvinistic nationalism, smothering religious dogmatism, pervasive commercialism, and the relentless interpellation to consume by the advertising and publicity industry. Baudelaire had begun to formulate this hero in Paris 25 years before Joyce. Haussmann's new boulevards were hacked and rammed through old city neighbourhoods, the city was drawn and quartered, and in the torturous process the rising bourgeoisie and the immiserated prolet-ariat came face to face with one another. Plate glass windows were all that separated the starving poor from the bright goods and fine dining.[6] In Baudelaire's time, Paris streets and passages were vibrant and alive with possibility and danger. To negotiate one's way through the chaos of modern life called for the emergence of the *flâneur*: a man of the crowd, but who had cultivated qualities of detachment and discernment, immersed in the currents of modern life, swept along despite his swimming against the tide, the object of prevailing powers and ideologies even though aware and conscious of those powers. The *flâneur* has an ambivalent and ironic sensibility; attuned to, and able to negotiate, ambiguity and paradox. The *flâneur* can read and understand the city. He has become a highly skilled hunter for meaning in the forest of signs – skills forged by sustained self-reflection from encounters with difference.

Similarly, Joyce's Bloom is formed by his heroic resistance to being levelled and swallowed by the huge impersonal forces of modern history. In *Ulysses* the objective culture against which Bloom is reflexively formed consists of the infinite might of the British Empire, as in Paris represented in Dublin by the Castle, the occupying garrison, and spectacular monuments of power like the statue of Nelson towering over the main thoroughfare. A walk across the city, which Stephen and Bloom do in *Ulysses*, involves a sustained encounter with objective culture and ideological interpellation. The British Empire, the Roman Catholic Church, the law, science, the mass media, the subaltern but mighty weight and moral authority of Irish Republicanism, the sentimental popular music and pulp fiction of the day that are woven seamlessly into the tapestry of commerce and consumption, comprising the ambience and the substance of a day's shopping, eating, and drinking in the city; these are the powers with which Joyce's Bloom must come to terms. In addition, Joyce's ideal type is self-reflexively formed by the encounter with the infinity of his own desires and anxieties; his own carnal appetites and erotic predilections welling up into his consciousness, his renegotiation of his intimate relations in the context of his wife's affair; and by the external power of the contingency of the social; people whom he runs into, some of whom he owes obligation to, some who are friends, some acquaintances, some strangers, some enemies. Bloom has to take care of himself, to maintain his integrity while negotiating his way through city life, and it is in this way that he is the heroic modern Ulysses: he navigates through the city even as he is menaced by its giants and seduced by its Sirens' songs.[7]

The risky, character-building dialectical encounter with the prevailing ideological powers is exemplified in Cyclops (Joyce, 1990, pp. 279–330), where Bloom comes face to face with nationalism and anti-Semitism directly and tangibly in an argument in a pub with the Citizen. The Citizen is a bar-stool patriot who spouts anti-imperialist revolutionary rhetoric, but whose nationalism is chauvinistic and xenophobic. The Citizen makes thinly veiled threats to Bloom, and when Bloom trumps his anti-Semitism by pointing out that Christ was a Jew, the incensed Citizen becomes violent. But Joyce's relationship to the ideology of militant Irish Republicanism is not as straightforward as it seems: Joyce has a deeply ambivalent and ambiguous relation to Irish nationalism. Parnell, the champion of Home Rule for Ireland by parliamentary means, was one of Joyce's heroes; many of his friends and associates were activists, amongst whom was Arthur Griffith, founder of Sinn Fein, to whom Bloom is represented as being a friend and adviser. Joyce was a supporter of the Sinn Fein movement and an admirer of Fenianism, but he saw Ireland ruled by Rome at least as much as by London, and he saw nationalism as a subaltern and neo-colonial reaction to power, and thus as a deformed extension of imperialism as much as a release from it (Deane, 1990, p. 44).

The Citizen is a critical portrayal of the one-eyed view of the world proffered by nationalism, but Joyce's critique is by no means specific to the peculiarities of nationalism: it extends to a wide range of other ideologies. Joyce's method for dealing with the hegemonic discourses of objective culture is comedic. While criticism is content merely to refute ideology, comedy has a more noble goal. Comedy seeks not only to challenge power but to reconcile it with its subjects, to cancel the opposition between them and collect the parties in a better humour. Joyce's comedy is that he identifies the lack underpinning all discourse, so that what had seemed to be sublimely powerful is shown to occupy the same profane world as everyone else. Power is revealed to be subject to discourse, and it becomes possible to negotiate and come to new terms with it rather than be simply subject to it. Joyce's method is that he identifies the characteristic ideological idiom of a wide variety of powers and accentuates them, showing each ideology to be in its own way formulaic, and thus to be an effect (and affect) of artifice and convention – an historically contingent discursive formation of articulated elements masquerading as a regime of truth, rather than the Truth itself.

In his caricature Joyce gives free rein to the Citizen's loquatiousness, so that he reveals himself eventually to be a bag of wind, much less threatening than he initially appears, and along the way, far from refuting the charges against the Empire made by the Citizen and his cronies, Joyce has Bloom endorse them. Joyce exposes the lack in the ideology of imperialism by playing up the pomposity of Empire, and then deflating it by profaning the sublime body of

Queen Victoria and other imperial heroes (she is depicted drunkenly pulling her gamekeeper into bed). Using a black parody of the Credo as a prayer to the barbarism of the Royal Navy, he alloys sedition with blasphemy, showing a profane equivalence between the sacred traditions of British militarism and Irish Catholicism.[8] He exposes the empty formalism of bourgeois parliamentary democracy by parodying verbose, rule-bound debate in the House of Commons, and by so doing he simultaneously reveals the lack in his own hero, Parnell, who was an acknowledged master of Parliamentary protocol, rhetoric and sophistry. He undermines the authority of Enlightenment rational discourse of science and law and their spurious claims to neutrality and objectivity by mimicking their ponderous jargons and putting their weighty pronouncements and judgements into the mouths of barflies. By having pub talk sound as authoritative as the voice of Science, Joyce shows, as Wittgenstein would hold, that science and law, like pub talk, are language games. They do not stand apart form the world, their truth claims are value-laden and contingent. By exaggerating to epic absurdity the pomp and circumstance and the theatricals of public culture – parades, theatre openings, a public execution, sporting events – Joyce ironises the sanctimonious, solemn rituals of church and state, the bombast and hyperbole of sports and popular journalism, the authoritative voice of the news, the vapidities and pretensions of the chattering classes in the society columns, and the self-aggrandising, conceited conventionalism of the cultural writers of the time. In this comedic context the Citizen's bigoted nationalism is pathetic and impotent – he 'waddle[s] to the door, puffing and blowing with the dropsy' (Joyce, 1990, p. 326) and throws an empty biscuit tin after Bloom.

The Citizen is a pale shade of the gigantic Cyclopean powers looming in the background: militarism, imperialism, one-eyed Nelson towering over the subaltern colonised city; the sharp, but narrow, relentless and inhuman gaze of science; the judgmental eagle eye of the law, the normalising panoptic gazes of Roman Catholicism and polite bourgeois society; and the vacuous, noisy, relentless culture industry. In Simmel's terms they constitute the burgeoning weight of objective culture, the hegemonic ideological discourses that crush Bloom's subjectivity. The Citizen is a representative of only one, albeit a significant aspect, of the problematic. If the Citizen ruled the city, Bloom would be killed. That is to say, if the city were ruled by any one of these powers – for they are each shown, one after the other in Joyce's comedic exposé, to be grotesque and totalitarian – then it would be impossible for any kind of freedom to exist in the city. But the Citizen doesn't rule. There are several competing powers, to which the Citizen and Bloom are equally subject,[9] and each of these powers is inherently flawed; they share a constitutive lack. The gaps and slippages between these competing powers, the shifting tectonic plates between empire and nation, science and religion, and the multiple overlapping webs of meaning and interrelations within which the encounter between Bloom and the Citizen are enmeshed – commerce and camaraderie, friendship and passing acquaintance, business and leisure, drunkenness and sobriety – form what Geertz calls 'piled-up structures of inference and implication' (Geertz, 1973, p. 7), the *mise en scène*, the webs of signification in which both Bloom and the Citizen are suspended: together, these constitute an unfathomable multiplicity of the sources of social action, and are the conditions of possibility of a practice of individual freedom and care of the self in modern Dublin, as they are also in Paris and Berlin.

In Bloom's encounter with the Citizen, Joyce shows us what is involved in the self-reflexive formation of principled relations to power. Joyce doesn't seek to 'refute' ideology by opposing it to science, nor does he seek to 'unmask' the truth that it occludes by criticism. Following Hegel, Joyce shows how self-consciousness is the 'return from otherness': the development of conscience – the integrity of identity in the face of the multiplicity of the social and its sovereign powers – grows from subjecting oneself 'to the infinity of the difference' (Hegel, 1977, pp. 107–108). Joyce doesn't ignore the Citizen, he has Bloom engage him in conversation. Contrary to revisionists who would erase the Citizen, by having Bloom engage with him – subject himself to the difference that he represents – Joyce collaborates with him, he lets him speak. The Citizen's opinion – and the kernel of truth in his opinion and in every *doxa*, every opinion, every discursive and ideological position – is given room in the conversation with Bloom. Thus Joyce preserves the otherness of the Other, providing Bloom and we readers with the opportunity of coming to terms with the Citizen and the ideological position he represents; we must listen to what he has to say, and in so doing we have the opportunity of self-reflexively coming to terms with the limits of our own subject positions.

Furthermore, in the encounter with Cyclops Joyce explores the flaws and the limits of his own modern hero, the uncreated consciousness that he is forging. Bloom appears in his exchange with the

Citizen as problematically equivocal. His reflexivity, his hermeneutic sensibility, leave him open to the charges of the nameless narrator (who is modelled on another of Joyce's heroes, his father)[10] that in wanting to cover all positions – Bloom interjects into his conversation with the Citizen the points of view of pacifism, humanism, Marxism, and feminism – he is left wanting a position for himself, that he has no position, that he is a half-and-half, and a good-for-nothing. Here Joyce is showing that there is no non-ideological position, no position outside of ideology, and to speak as though there were is to delude oneself and also to risk being groundless and antisocial. Bloom shares the same problem as Socrates: the city may decide that it has no use for the man who is sceptical of all prevailing ideologies, who prioritises thought over action and doubt over certainty, who wants to work out truth – that is, to reveal the lack underpinning all truth claims – through discussing all points of view. The *aporia* that this questioning and seeking understanding produces interferes with action and practical life. And later in *Ulysses*, in a hallucinogenic sequence in Circe, Bloom imagines himself sharing Socrates' fate (Joyce, 1990, pp. 449–451).

This condition of coexistence with multiple Others, of mutually and self-reflexively negotiating the manifold encounters with alterity, forms the collective and individual existential conditions of the modern city. Joyce's Bloom is the ideal type (and, Joyce intends, the prototype) of a subject who occupies the paradoxical modern subject position of permanent liminality (Szakolczai, 1999), of existing in a condition of perpetual transition, always travelling, but never arriving. In Bloom, Joyce makes a value and a principle of being the place-holder of the condition of permanent liminality, and thus transforms the terrible fate of modern subjectivity into its most beautiful and enduring form. This is the ontological and ethical significance of Joyce's *flâneur*: Bloom's *jouissance* is to endure the existential condition of permanent liminality: he makes himself at home with the condition of transcendental homelessness. Bloom is the subjective correspondent of what Lefort identifies as the radical symbolic mutation of power instituted by the democratic revolution, where power becomes an empty place (Lefort, 1988). As the indeterminate, the wanderer, the Jew, the protean stranger, Bloom is the decentred subject who corresponds with the decentring of power; he is place-holder of the constitutive antagonism of the social,[11] the persistence of the Real that assures the radical unfixity and indeterminacy of social relations, and thus the Utopian moment of openness and the promise of futurity in the uncontrollable adventure of democratic life.[12]

By systematically placing himself in the position of permanent liminality Bloom's practice of care of the self represents a spirited way of being in the city, as Hegel understands a spirited form of life:

> ... the life of Spirit is not the life that shrinks from death and keeps itself untouched by devastation, but rather the life that endures it and maintains itself in it. It wins its truth only when, in utter dismemberment, it finds itself. This tarrying with the negative is the magical power that converts it into being. (Hegel, 1977, quoted in Žižek, 1993)

Bloom is an advertising canvasser, and as such he is acutely aware and tuned in to his interpellation in the commercial life of the city. Because it is his livelihood, he is thoroughly familiar with the idiom and the imaginative structure of commercial interpellation, and – because he depends on it to make his living – it is simultaneously a source of security and insecurity to him. So much does he understand the world of advertising that he interprets and critiques it, and can enjoy it and evade it, all the time with a sharp eye for his own professional opportunity. Like Ulysses, a musician himself, he wants to listen to the Sirens' songs, so in spite of the dangers that he is fully aware of, far from avoiding the Sirens he ties himself to the mast, and sails through them with ears wide open. It is Bloom's sustained tarrying with the negative that forms him as exemplary subject. Lacan calls Joyce 'le sinthome Joyce': 'St Thom.' (St Thomas Aquinas), from whom Joyce borrows the formula of the epiphany – that the truth that gives unity to the world flares out in the mundane (and for Lacan that the truth of the subject – the lack, the subject's decentredness – is written in the symptom, for those who have eyes to see), and 'saint homme', the saintly man who, though existentially vulnerable, heroically commits himself to tarrying with the negative, and risks spiritual devastation and dismemberment to come close enough to bear witness to the Real: for it is also the task of the saint faithfully to record the epiphanies and thereby to reveal the (real) truth of the world: that is the lack, the constitutive antagonism of the social, and the radical contingency of prevailing ideologies, discourses, regimes of truth, that makes power always subject to discourse. And while this is an onerous responsibility, a spirited relation to the city is joyous and playful, for Joyce is also *jouis*, play, joy, and the good form Joyce shows us in his phenomenology of the metropolis is by his playful attuning to its *jouissance*.

The Utopian ideal represented by Bloom as prototypical new man that contemporary people might try to live up to is the ideal of understanding. And in this, Joyce agrees with Simmel, when he says that the forms and contents of life in the metropolis are such that 'a judge-like attitude on our part is inappropriate ... it is our task neither to complain nor to condone, but only to understand' (Simmel, 1971, p. 339). Bloom represents a further refinement to the care of the self of the blasé cosmopolitan and the *flâneur*, a capacity for *verstehen* (Weber, 1968), understanding. Bloom exemplifies a hermeneutic sensibility, a willingness, a cultivated capacity, and a commitment to see the world from other people's point(s) of view. Like Socrates, on whom he is to a great extent modelled, Joyce's Bloom knows that the world opens itself up differently to everyone according to their position in it; and that the 'sameness' of the world, its commonness ... or 'objectivity' (as we would say from the subjective viewpoint of modern philosophy) resides in the fact that the same world opens up to everyone and that despite all differences between men and their positions in the world – and consequently their *doxai* (opinions) – 'both you and I are human' (Arendt, 1990, pp. 80, 73–103). Like Socrates, Joyce's Bloom represents the good of trying to understand the diverse ways in which the same reality appears to different people, and trying to reconcile opposing views and diverse realities with one another. He systematically and deliberately tries to understand others, that is to put himself in their shoes, to see the world from their point of view. This is what makes Bloom's *flâneur* an heroic *Übermensch*, a better human being. Bloom tries to combine many lives of others in his own, but at the same time he does not lose himself in their otherness, and neither does he claim to fully understand and represent the others' views; he allows others their otherness. Bloom is the subjective embodiment of the Greek principle of *phronesis* (political insight). Bloom is the *phronomous*, the understanding man whose insight into the world of human affairs qualifies him for leadership in the city, though not of course to rule it (Arendt, 1990, pp. 75–76). The problem that Bloom faces, that of negotiating a principled path through the various ideological powers that beset us in modern life, is everyone's problem. Hence H.C.E. (here comes everybody) of *Finnegans Wake*; and the perennial and intractable nature of the problem of dealing with ideology is what gives *Ulysses* its universal import. Bloom is an ideal-type hermeneutic actor, who tries to see the world from many, changing points of view. He is divided and Protean himself: a stranger, a *flâneur*, an insider and an outsider to discourses of empire, nation, church and commerce; an ad-man, a civic-minded private man, a womanly man, a man who even tries to see things from a blind man's point of view. The multitudes of views represented in *Ulysses* are always partial and imperfect. Joyce himself is partially sighted. Aren't we all similarly handicapped? Such are the limits that the human condition places on knowledge/power, tempering it towards irony and wisdom.

NOTES

1. The *flâneur* appears throughout Benjamin's writings, in the *Passagenwerk*, on Baudelaire, and is a simulacrum of Benjamin himself in works like *One Way Street* (1979), *Moscow Dairies* (1986), and *Berlin Chronicle* (1970). For a succinct formulation see Benjamin (1995).
2. For a fuller exposition of the themes of this essay see Simmel (1990).
3. On a related theme see Žižek's discussion of the wreck of the Titanic, in Žižek (1989).
4. For an introductory history of Temple Bar see Liddy (1992).
5. For a good account of urban renewal in Dublin and the revitalisation of Temple Bar, see Corcoran (1998).
6. For an excellent discussion of this process in Baudelaire's Paris, see Berman (1998, pp. 131–171).
7. I owe this insight to Professor Arpad Szakolczai, National University of Ireland, Cork.
8.
   They believe in rod, the scourger almighty, creator of hell upon earth, and in Jacky Tar, the son of a gun, who was conceived of unholy boast, born of the fighting navy, suffered under rump and dozen, was scarified, flayed and curried, yelled like bloody hell, the third day he arose again from the bed, steered into haven and sittethed on his beam end til further orders whence he shall come to drudge for a living and be paid (Joyce, 1990, p. 314).

9. For this point, and for other insights on this paper, I am indebted to Professor Kieran Bonner, University of Waterloo, Canada.
10. On this, see Richard Ellmann's definitive biography of Joyce (Ellmann, 1982, p. 22).
11. The phrase 'constitutive antagonism of the social' is coined by Ernesto Laclau and Chantal Mouffe (1985).
12. For an elaboration and exposition of this theme, see Mouffe (1989).

REFERENCES

Arendt, H. (1990) 'Philosophy and Politics', *Social Research*, vol. 57, no. 1, pp. 73–103.

Benjamin, W. (1995) 'Paris: Capital of the Nineteenth Century' in Kasanitz, P. (ed.) *Metropolis: Centre and Symbol of our Time* (New York: Macmillan).

Berman, M. (1998) *All that is Solid Melts into Air* (New York: Penguin).

Buck-Morss, S. (1995) *The Dialectics of Seeing: Walter Benjamin and the Arcades Project* (Cambridge, Mass.: MIT Press).

Corcoran, M. (1998) 'The Re-enchantment of Temple Bar', in Peillon M. and Slater, E. (eds) *Encounters with Modern Ireland* (Dublin: Institute of Public Administration).

Deane, S. (1990) *Nationalism, Colonialism, and Literature* (Minneapolis: University of Minnesota Press).

Ellmann, R. (1982) *James Joyce* (Oxford: Oxford University Press).

Foucault, M. (1990) *The History of Sexuality, vol. III, The Care of the Self* (New York: Vintage).

Foucault, M. (1998) 'The Ethic of the Care of the Self as a Practice of Freedom' in Bernauer J. and Rasmussen D. (eds) *The Final Foucault* (Cambridge, Mass.: MIT Press).

Geertz, C. (1973) *The Interpretation of Cultures* (New York: Basic Books).

Hegel G.W.F. (1977) *The Phenomenology of Spirit* (Oxford: Oxford University Press).

Joyce, J. (1987) *A Portrait of the Artist as a Young Man* (New York: Penguin).

Joyce, J. (1990) *Ulysses* (New York: Vintage).

Laclau, E. and Mouffe, C. (1985) *Hegemony and Social Strategy* (London: Verso).

Lefort, C. (1988) *Democracy and Political Theory* (Cambridge: Polity).

Liddy, P. (1992) *Temple Bar Dublin: An Illustrated History* (Dublin: Temple Bar Properties Ltd).

Mouffe, C. (1989) 'Radical Democracy: Modern or Postmodern?', in Ross, A. (ed.) *Universal Abandon?* (Minneapolis: University of Minnesota Press).

Simmel, G. (1971) 'The Metropolis and Mental Life', in Levine, D. (ed.) *Georg Simmel: On Individuality and Social Forms* (Chicago: University of Chicago Press).

Simmel, G. (1990) *The Philosophy of Money* (London: Routledge).

Szakolczai, A. (1999) *Reflexive Historical Sociology* (London: Routledge).

Weber, M. (1968) *Economy and Society, I-II* (New York: Bedminster Press).

Žižek, S. (1989) *The Sublime Object of Ideology* (London: Verso).

Žižek, S. (1993) *Tarrying with the Negative: Kant, Hegel, and the Critique of Ideology* (Durham: Duke University Press).

PART II

Ideology vs. Poststructuralism

5 Rehabilitating Ideology after Poststructuralism

Siniša Malešević

Until quite recently, the concept of ideology was considered to be indispensable in the study of social and political life. Sociologists, political scientists, social and political theorists, anthropologists, social psychologists, as well as those researching cultural studies, have extensively applied this concept in their work and the only point of divergence and disagreement was, as always, different conceptual understandings of what ideology is. For some, mostly political scientists, ideologies were always discussed in the plural, meaning different sets of ideas and principles about the possible or desirable organisation of particular societies (as in liberalism, conservatism, socialism or environmentalism), while others, notably sociologists, have tended to speak of ideology in the singular, viewing it as a set of ideas or practices related to a specific structural organisation of society (as in Marx's 'fetishism of commodities', Engels's 'false consciousness' or Žižek's 'fantasy of enjoyment'). Although significantly different, neither of these traditions and approaches has questioned the relevance of the concept of ideology. Poststructuralism was the first theoretical movement to reject the entire notion of ideology, viewing it as totalistic, essentialist and methodologically and theoretically obsolete. Poststructuralism has been particularly critical of the way ideology was used in the writings of its ancestors – that is, structuralists.

This chapter aims to critically review and analyse the way the concept of ideology was and is used in structuralism and poststructuralism, as well as to defend and rehabilitate the concept of ideology from poststructuralist attacks. It is argued that the theory and concept of ideology can be rescued as a valuable research tool by recognising and accommodating some of the pitfalls identified by poststructuralist approaches without accepting the radical relativism of some poststructuralist positions. The chapter is divided into three sections. In the first section, structuralist approaches to ideology are briefly discussed and critically elaborated. In the second section, various poststructuralist criticisms of ideology are presented and criticised. The last section maps an outline for the new concept and theory of ideology.

STRUCTURALIST APPROACHES TO IDEOLOGY

In order to deal properly with the poststructuralist approaches to ideology it is necessary to examine their ancestors, that is the structuralist views on ideology. There are basically three different and mutually opposing structuralist traditions – Marxist, functionalist and anthropological structuralism.

Marxist structuralism is usually associated with the work of Althusser, but different variants of Marxist structuralism are also evident in the early works of Hirst (critical structuralism), Goldmann (genetic structuralism) and Godelier (economic structuralism) (Malešević, 2002). The common characteristic of Marxist structuralism is its emphasis on the state and economy. The state is seen as the principal agent of action and the concept of ideology is employed exclusively in reference to the state power. Structuralist Marxists follow classical Marxism in their perception of the state as an instrument of repression, but they differ from agency-centred Marxism in downplaying the role of class struggle at the expense of structural determinants (e.g. capitalism) which are found to be central for the analysis of ideology.

For Althusser class hegemony is achieved not only through Repressive State Apparatuses such as military, police, courts but primarily through Ideological State Apparatuses – education system, mass media, family or church. He argues that 'no class can hold State power over a long period of time without at the same time exercising its hegemony over and in the State Ideological Apparatuses' (Althusser, 1994, p. 112).

Furthermore, ideology is built into the material apparatuses that are determined by the relations of production – i.e. capitalist economy. For structural Marxists ideology has a tangible, material form which is not only completely independent of individual subjectivity but is also able to create and mould subjects. As Althusser claims (1994, p. 125), ideology is 'not the system of the real relations which govern the existence of individuals, but the imaginary relation of those individuals to the real relations in which they live'. For structuralist Marxists, human beings are constituted by ideology, while ideology itself originates from the particular type of production in society – capitalism. In other words, the capitalist state hegemony is maintained through ideological state apparatuses, which are themselves tied to the dominant modes of production in a particular (capitalist) society. Structuralist Marxists also strongly oppose ideology and science. For Althusser, for example, ideology is abstract while science is concrete; ideology is historically contingent while science is ahistoric; ideology is only raw material while science is exact and accurate. Althusser sees his structuralist Marxism as a form of science *par excellence* and claims that the role of science is to creatively use and criticise the products of ideology.

Functionalist structuralism shares with its Marxist counterpart the emphasis on the collective roots of ideology as well as the perception of ideology as something that stands in opposition to science. Malinowski, Shils, Parsons and Sartori all define ideology with reference to dominant social institutions – the school, the family, the state. They all also make a strong distinction between closed, dogmatic and stable concepts associated with ideology, and open, flexible and prone-to-change values seen as non-ideological.

However, unlike Marxism, structuralist functionalism ignores the economy and materialist explanations of ideology. In this tradition ideology is seen as a normative value system necessary for social cohesion and the proper functioning of societies. For Malinowski (1926), ideology/myth is a sacred tale that functions as a practical justification of relationships and practices existing in the particular society. For Shils (1968), ideologies are no more than normative belief systems that are founded on 'systematic intellectual constructs' that demand total commitment of their followers. For Parsons (1991, p. 39), ideology is 'an evaluative, i.e. value-loaded existential statement about the actual or prospective state of a given social system or type or category of social system'. In Sartori's theory (1969) ideology is more precisely identified with the 'political part of a belief system' and is tied to strong affects and closed cognitive structure.

Although functionalist structuralism relates ideology strongly to society, looking at its collectivist origins, unlike Marxism it does not perceive this relationship as being conflictual. Ideology is not viewed as something being imposed upon human beings, but rather as a functional necessity without which society cannot exist. Ideologies do not shape, structure or *interpellate* and thus manipulate individuals as in Althusser, but are rather seen as 'building blocks' for the integration of societies.

Anthropological structuralism of Lévi-Strauss and Barthes shares with Marxists and functionalists their understanding of ideology as a macrostructural phenomenon. Just like Marxism, anthropological structuralists aim at discovering 'hidden' structures behind more manifest actions and similarly to functionalists their goal is to demonstrate the necessity of ideology in every society. However, unlike Marxists they are only sporadically (Barthes) or not at all (Lévi-Strauss) interested in the modes of production and the role that capitalism plays in the formation of ideologies, and unlike functionalists they are not concerned with the integrative role of ideology in society. Their main aim is to apply the methods of linguistics (e.g. structural analysis) to social relations. For anthropological structuralists, myths and ideologies are no more than logical models that aim at overcoming a contradiction between nature and culture and as such they function independently from individual consciousness. In the words of Lévi-Strauss (1975, p. 12) the aim of structural analysis is not 'to show how men think in myths, but how myths operate in men's minds without them being aware of the fact'.

For Barthes (1972) and Lévi-Strauss there is no significant difference between ideological/mythical contents and other contents; they all operate in a similar way, have similar pattern structure and apply identical logical principles. Anthropological structuralists use structural analysis with the simple aim of identifying the elementary logical structure on which message, myth, ritual or any other meaningful content is based. Lévi-Strauss aims to discover the common structural forms and common logical patterns behind arbitrary symbols and randomness that are present in myths and ideologies. He looks for what he calls *mythemes*, that is the elementary units of myth, with the aim of identifying the logical order behind myth's formal structure. Lévi-Strauss has little interest in the actual contents of the particular myths and ideologies. What is important to demonstrate and explain is the similarity between the structure of different myths and ideologies.

Although different, these three structuralist approaches to ideology share several important common features. All three assign the overwhelming primacy to structure over agency in the explanation of ideology. All three perceive human will and individual consciousness as largely irrelevant in the explanation of ideology. All three argue for an ahistorical theory of ideology. All three share the view that with the right methodology one can successfully and precisely differentiate between ideological and non-ideological forms of knowledge.

The classical criticisms of structuralism have successfully challenged all of these claims. It has often been convincingly argued that human beings are much more than just bearers of social roles and that regardless of how powerful ideologies are there is always room for autonomous individual action. As Pareto (1966) was already aware, ideologies cannot run against already existing human sentiments. To use his language, derivations can intensify residues but they cannot manufacture them. The residues have to be there in the first place in order to be instrumentalised. Ideologies cannot work *ex nihilo*. In addition, as Gouldner (1970) and more recently Giddens (1991) and Beck (1991) have convincingly argued, human beings are also self-reflexive creatures. Very often, they are aware of the entire process of ideological interpellation and are still taking part in it, or are simply adjusting in accordance with their own interests, values and emotions.

Critics have also pointed out that ideologies always originate within a particular geographical and historical environment. Although all communist states derived their official ideologies from Lenin's interpretations of Marx and Engels, each society had a particular and unique brand of its own state-sponsored communist ideology, which took into consideration particularities of the national history, history of its own communist movement, differences in the economic, cultural and political development of the particular society, and so on. It was also very often the case that these differences (perceived by outsiders as insignificant) were central for the legitimisation of the particular regime, as was the case with Yugoslav self-management socialism, Polish nationalist communism and Chinese Maoism. Structuralist preference of 'synchronic' over 'diachronic' analysis leaves these substantial and often crucial differences out of its explanation.

However, most criticism was placed against the structuralist claim of having developed scientific, meaning non-ideological, tools for the study of ideology. Although structuralism opposes the positivist ambition to explain phenomena only in terms of immediately observable entities, and abandons the search for the laws of causality, it too is a victim of overoptimistic scientism. Its aim, to uncover the latent structures of manifest phenomena with the help of structural analysis, is even more arbitrary than the methods of positivist social science. If one cannot rely on the strict procedures of laboratory experimentation, sampling, surveying, factor or regression analysis, why would one trust the extreme arbitrariness of the 'synchronic analysis'? In addition, as many critics have emphasised, the linguistic methods are hardly applicable for the study of the complexity of social life. As Giddens (1987, p. 200) rightly argues, 'linguistics cannot provide a model for analysing the nature of either agency or social institutions, because it is in a basic sense only explicable through an understanding of these'.

Other types of criticism, such as those coming from the Frankfurt school sociologists, show that even when knowledge is completely reduced to its technical forms, it is still far from being non-ideological or value-free. As Marcuse (1971, p. 130) points out, 'domination perpetuates and extends itself not only through technology but as technology, and the latter provides the great legitimisation of the expanding political power, which absorbs all spheres of culture'.

However, the most severe criticism of structuralist approaches to ideology is to be found in the writings of poststructuralist authors, some of whom grew up intellectually within the tradition of Marxist or anthropological structuralism. Let us take a brief look at how post-structuralism views the concept of ideology.

POSTSTRUCTURALISM AND IDEOLOGY

Although leading poststructuralist approaches differ on many points they agree on one thing – they all firmly reject the concept of ideology. For Foucault (1980, p. 118) the concept of ideology cannot have any analytical relevance because (a) it is based on true/false criteria; (b) it overemphasises the role of conscious subjects; and (c) it is viewed as secondary reality (superstructure) that is regularly determined by the economic base. According to Foucault, knowledge and power are deeply related, since the use of power always produces new information and novel types of knowledge. He argues that since 'no power can be exercised without extraction, appropriation, distribution or retention of knowledge' therefore 'power and knowledge imply one another' (Foucault 1977, p. 27). Because of this peculiar power–knowledge relationship, ideology cannot be, as in the Marxist tradition, opposed to science. Ideology and science cannot be analysed and assessed in the light of a true/false criterion. As 'truth' in itself is situational and historically and geographically contingent and at the same time always tied to power, there are no universally accepted rationalist parameters to distinguish 'truth' from 'non-truth'. These parameters lie at all times in the realm of a particular concrete community. Instead of ideology Foucault operates with the concept of discourse. In his view discourses are much less totalistic and universalistic than the concept of ideology as used in structuralism. Discourses operate on a much lower level of generality and are not evaluated using true/false dichotomy. Unlike ideology, this concept is used in order to understand and explain how particular ideas and practices relate to the context, which has 'its own history and conditions of existence'. What is crucial for Foucault is not whether the ideas and practices expressed within a particular normative discourse are provable, but rather how they operate in relation to power.

Baudrillard (1988) and Lyotard (1984) follow similar lines of thinking. They both oppose the analytical relevance of the concept of ideology. For Baudrillard we live in a postmodern world of isolated individual actions devolved of any intrinsic meaning, incoherent and incomprehensible social events and fragmented and fractured realities. This postmodern world does not depend on modes of production, industrial growth and economics, but predominantly on the production, use and exchange of images, signs, and information. However, these images, signs and information are not produced, exchanged and consumed in the same way as material goods once were, to secure a new and better reality. They are rather seen by Baudrillard as simulations that have lost their original meanings and now do not reveal anything beyond the 'real'. In his view there is no reality any more; everything has become an extensive simulation. Instead of reality we live in hyperreality which can easily be and is falsified by different and often opposing representations.

Just like Foucault, Baudrillard does not believe in the autonomy of conscious subjects and prefers the idea of discourse over that of ideology. However, discourses in Baudrillard have little analytical strength; they are only empty images – simulacra. The problem of ideology critique for Baudrillard is that its aim is always the same – 'to restore the objective process' – and he argues that 'it is always a false problem to want to restore the truth beneath the simulacrum. This is ultimately why power is so in accord with ideological discourses and discourses on ideology, for these are all discourses of truth – always good' (Baudrillard, 1988, p. 182).

Lyotard also thinks that in the postmodern world there is no place for individual subjects. Following Wittgenstein he views society as a sequence of language games where one can see only dissolved social subjects. According to Lyotard, in the postmodern world there is no place for the single universalist Enlightenment-generated concept of Reason, but only for many different, mutually incommensurable unprivileged reasons. He opposes any attempt towards totality and ridicules universalist rationalist conceptions that promise comprehensive positive explanation and hence emancipation and salvation. These theories and explanations which focus on and give privilege to singular 'essential' identities such as nation, gender, race or class are described as 'totalitarian meta-narratives' and are resolutely rejected. Consequently, there is no place for ideology critique in his position: all language games are equal and legitimate.

The post-Marxism of Laclau and Mouffe (1985) also shares many similarities with Foucault's, Baudrillard's and Lyotard's criticisms of ideology. Laclau and Mouffe also identify the concept of ideology with its Marxist derivative and intend to show the weaknesses of this position. They agree with poststructuralists that classical Marxist analyses reduce plurality and difference by attributing a privileged role to the proletariat and treat social identities as stable and fixed. They argue that social identities are fundamentally relational and situational. Like other post-essentialists, they believe that there are no privileged historical subjects, whether these be classes, nations or something else. Accordingly, no social relations between individuals or between groups are necessarily of a permanent, universal or continuous nature. As a result, Laclau and Mouffe also opt for the concept of discourse over that of ideology.

Nevertheless, their concept of discourse differs significantly from those of Foucault, Lyotard and Baudrillard. They define discourse as a 'structured totality resulting from the articulatory practice', where an articulatory practice is 'any practice establishing a relation among elements such that their identity is modified as a result of the articulatory practice' (Laclau and Mouffe, 1985, p. 105). As is evident, their understanding of discourse is much broader and more totalising than in poststructuralism.

For Laclau and Mouffe all social actions are discursively constructed. Discourses just like identities are also relational. They argue that individuals are dispersed by and within different discursive formations. Since individual subjects change their social positions and their relations to the discourse, formations are never eternally fixed. For Laclau and Mouffe they are only 'partial fixations'. In their view 'any discourse is constituted as an attempt to dominate the field of discursivity, to arrest the flow of differences, to construct a centre'

(Laclau and Mouffe, 1985, p. 112). Furthermore, they argue that owing to the fact that objects are always constituted as objects of – and in – a particular discourse, one cannot distinguish between discursive and non-discursive practices. Following Gramsci and Foucault, they also ascribe to discourses a value of materiality. In other words the practices of articulation have their material dimension: institutions, organisations, ritualistic practices, techniques, and so on. However, this materiality of discourses is not in any significant way connected to the consciousness of the subjects. Positions of the subjects are, rather, dispersed within a discursive formation. In the eyes of Laclau and Mouffe, society, as a stable articulated entity, does not exist. What one can observe are only perpetual attempts of discursive articulation.

The common features of poststructuralist approaches can be summarised in the following three points: (a) they all renounce the entire concept of ideology and operate with alternative concepts such as 'discourses', 'simulacras', 'language games' or 'meta-narratives'; (b) they all rebuff true/false or science/non-science criteria in distinguishing between different social actions, viewing all knowledge claims as discursive, relative, situational and therefore equal; and (c) they all stand firmly against essentialism, positivism and universalism.

However, although poststructuralism appears to be extremely critical of the structuralist concepts of ideology, it is still unable to overcome many of its shortcomings. Firstly, even though poststructuralism launches fierce criticism of the concept of ideology, as some have already observed (e.g. Larrain, 1994, p. 292), it reintroduces this concept through the back door, thus contradicting itself. As Larrain (1994, p. 292) states 'while they [poststructuralists] doubt the validity of total discourses and of their ideological critique they must assume the validity of their own critique of total discourses'. This criticism is of course derived from the much wider problem that concerns poststructuralist understanding of knowledge and truth. As Habermas (1987, p. 247), Taylor (1984, pp. 175–177), Bevir (1999, p. 70) and others have pointed out, in rejecting the possibility of individual freedom and reason, poststructuralists cut the ground from under their own feet. In other words, the ethical criticisms of meta-narratives, language games and discourses are undermined when there is no epistemological or normative 'axis' to build upon.

This radical epistemological relativism is not only ethically problematic, because it does not (want to) differentiate between different types of power, thus (unintentionally) equating for example sexual inequality and genocide, but more importantly for this study, it is analytically insufficient. Its methodology applies no appropriate criteria in distinguishing between different 'regimes of truth'. How can one distinguish between meta-narrative and non-meta-narrative? In order to move from the metaphoric level of analysis towards useful empirical analysis of the 'regimes of truth', one has to offer better criteria on how one is to decide that particular discourses are incommensurable. Poststructuralism does not offer us an adequate conceptual apparatus that could be used in the empirical research. As a result, most poststructuralist analyses remain on the level of statement, metaphor or extensive description. The main question here is certainly how to overcome the arbitrariness of poststructuralist methodology.

This arbitrariness is perhaps most visible in the way concepts such as 'power' are used in Foucault's writings. The statement that power is everywhere is analytically flawed. In social sciences when attempting to explain a particular social phenomenon we introduce concepts in order to organise our information in a meaningful way, with an aim to differentiate those events and actions that we find somehow more relevant, from the rest. When we say that power is everywhere, we automatically say that power is nowhere. By relativising our concepts we are unable to provide explanations. One can agree with Foucault that micro or local dimensions of power are exceptionally important for understanding of social life, but this should not prevent us from differentiating, studying or finding that the macro state power can have wider and deeper impact on human condition. Furthermore, as argued and documented by Fox (1998, p. 424), while poststructuralism may be able to provide research tools for the analysis of 'relatively unresisting subjectivities' (such as in Foucault's analysis of prisoners and patients in mental hospitals), this approach lacks conceptual tools for analysis of 'the conditions under which resistance to power becomes possible, why some people resist and others do not, and how resistance may be successful'.

There is another problem with the poststructuralist position that has both ethical and analytical implications. By stating that every society or group has its own regime of truth, we deny the possibility of individual choice within a group. The problem of cultural relativism is its insensitivity towards particularities within the particular. In other words, by assuming that a certain group of people or society share the same 'regime of truth', one remains totalist on the level of the particular. Is a macro meta-narrative any less 'totalitarian' than a micro meta-narrative?

Secondly, the preference for the concepts of 'discourse', 'language games', 'simulacra' or 'meta-narratives' over that of ideology does not solve the problem that exists in structuralist writings. On the one hand, it makes little difference whether we use concepts such as 'ideology', 'myth' or 'discourses' if our aims remains the same – to show that somebody else's views are less (or at least no more) true than ours. Although poststructuralists distance themselves from such an aim they too are engaged in the activity of delegitimising other perspectives describing them as a 'meta-narratives' or 'discourses'. On the other hand, the concept of 'discourse' is very often used in an extremely imprecise and vague sense, meaning everything and nothing. For example, Laclau and Mouffe (1985) recognise that it is impossible to make a distinction between discursive and non-discursive practices. Some writers use the concept of discourse only to refer to a particular set of ideas, views or values (e.g. Baudrillard and Lyotard) while others, such as the later Foucault, or Laclau and Mouffe, include in it much more (such as practices and actions). Hence, when the concept refers only to ideas, values and meanings, we end up with a classical idealism that argues that human action is governed and shaped primarily by discourses and only secondarily by interests. When it include practices, actions, rituals, etc. (i.e. the body instead of consciousness) we end up with a more materialist theory of 'discourses' that in the long run does not differ much from the Althusserian project. In other words, although poststructuralists prefer discourse over ideology, when they are forced to specify the meaning of the discourse in a concrete analysis, the concept of the discourse differs little from that of ideology.

As in structuralism, we can read in Foucault, or Laclau and Mouffe, that 'discourses constitute the subject', that 'subjects are not the producers of discourse but rather "positions" in discourse which can be occupied by any individual' (Foucault 1977, p. 115), and so on. If we replace the word 'discourse' with 'ideology' or 'myth' these sentences sound just as if they were taken from Althusser's or Lévi-Strauss's works.

To conclude, poststructuralist attempts to overcome the deficiencies of the structuralist concept of ideology are far from successful. Even though postructuralism rightly challenges the totalist ambitions, hard essentialism and scientism of structuralist

approaches, it fails to provide a better theoretical and methodological apparatus for the study of ideology.

IDEOLOGY AFTER POSTSTRUCTURALISM

In an article published in 1987, Giddens launched a sharp criticism
of both structuralism and poststructuralism; the first line reads:
'Structuralism, and post-structuralism also, are dead traditions of
thought' (Giddens, 1987, p. 195). In the last two decades we have
witnessed largely the opposite – the late 1980s and 1990s as well as
the beginning of this century have witnessed an unprecedented proliferation of books, studies and journal articles written from the
poststructuralist or postmodernist perspective. Even structuralism
had its significant revival. The end of the cold war and the total
collapse of the communist world further rejuvenated poststructuralist thought, demonstrating the death of another great
meta-narrative of the Enlightenment project – Marxism-Leninism.
If poststructuralism was a still largely marginal movement in the
early and mid-1980s, it has certainly become mainstream now.
Today no serious academic will so easily dismiss poststructuralist or
postmodernist ideas. In fact, even Giddens's more recent work on
reflexive modernisation (1991, 1992) incorporates many poststructuralist ideas, perhaps without being aware of the fact.

Hence, poststructuralist criticisms of scientism, universalism and
hard essentialism, as developed in various 'modernist' approaches
(including their criticism of the concept of ideology), cannot be so
easily dismissed. Poststructuralism rightly challenges the totalising
ambitions of ideology critique. It is really as difficult in today's world
to attribute a special and privileged role to one single social actor
(e.g. class, nation, gender, race or community) as it is to one meta-
narrative. For example, a Marxist concept of ideology, with its focus
on economy, capitalism and the modes of production can hardly
operate in societies where the economy does not exist as an independent realm, as is the case with communist and other centrally
planned regimes. Furthermore, by locating the origins of ideology
in the development of modes of production and class struggle only,
Marxist explanations ignore the evidence of historical and political
research that relates the birth of ideology to the emergence of
modernity and the development of modern bureaucratic nation
states. Similarly, the rigid opposition of science and ideology as
maintained in anthropological and functionalist structuralism
cannot stand the scrutiny of empirical research, and it looks obsolete

in this day and age when the status of the natural sciences themselves has become highly questionable. Poststructuralism is very convincing indeed in demonstrating that the basis for having narratives with privileged agents of social change is quite weak and that reality in itself is both multiple and discursive.

However, recognising the notion that there are no universally privileged social actors does not mean accepting the view that all 'language games' are equal and that social actions of all actors have equivalent impact on social relations. On the contrary, by acknowledging the idea that there are no general and omnipresent social actors one can better focus on particularly shaped asymmetrical relations of power. One can now concentrate on the questions of when, why and how interpretations and articulations of social reality by these particularly privileged social agents become hegemonic, shared or trusted by many. In other words, although 'meta-narratives', 'discourses', 'simulacras' and 'language games' might be epistemologically of equal worth, their structural position (i.e. whether any particular discourse or meta-narrative is dominant and institutionalised or not) makes them structurally and ontologically very different and unequal.

Because of this structural inequality and the existing asymmetrical relations of power in everyday life, one should not so easily reject the concept of ideology in the social sciences. The concept of ideology still has many advantages over the concepts of 'discourse' or 'meta-narrative'. Nevertheless, in order to accommodate criticism put forward by poststructuralists, it is important to specify what the concept of ideology should stand for.

First of all, it is necessary to point out that poststructuralist criticism operates with the concept of ideology inherited from the Marxist structuralism. In the poststructuralist view, ideology, as Barrett (1991) puts it, focuses on the 'economics of un-truth' whereas 'discourse analysis' deals with the 'politics of truth'. Foucault (1980, p. 118) and Baudrillard (1988, p. 182) have both explicitly stated that they are against 'ideological analysis' because 'it always stands in virtual opposition to something else which is supposed to count as truth' or 'it is always a false problem to want to restore the truth beneath the simulacrum'. However by reducing the concept of ideology to its Marxist variant, they have failed to account properly for the contributions of other theoretical traditions.

The concept of ideology cannot be equated with its structuralist and Marxist versions because there are many other traditions of inquiry that have developed the concept of ideology, such as the psychoanalytic tradition (Freud's 'illusion', 'delusion' and 'justification', Reich's 'political rationalisation of sadism', Žižek's 'enjoyment and lack'), the classical elite theory of Pareto ('derivations') and Mosca ('political formulae'), Sorel's political myth, the cultural approach of Geertz ('ideology as a cultural system') and Mannheim ('ideology and utopia'), the Weberianism of Boudon ('rationality of ideology'), Critical Theory ('science and technology as ideology') and so on. Drawing on some of these approaches, particularly Weberianism and classical elite theory, one is able to develop a theory of ideology that can incorporate positive features of poststructuralist criticism such as rejection of the application of the crude true/false and science/non-science dichotomies to the study of ideology, as well as poststructuralist criticism of meta-narratives, without reinstating extreme relativism, analytical and intellectual paralysis (Malešević, 2002).

The new theory of ideology should be capable of reconciling the explanatory merits of ideology theories with the ideas and critique of poststructuralism. However, this attempt raises a number of problems, of which the most important is the question: is it possible to renounce positivism, universalism and attempts to build a grand metatheory and at the same time maintain an explanatorily oriented concept of ideology?

This can be achieved only if the concept of ideology is reformulated and removed from its Marxist obsession with the 'economics of untruth', its structuralist obsession with the latent and manifest patterns, its poststructuralist radical relativism, obsessed with the 'celebration of differences', and the obsession of all three with the structure and the macro level of analysis. In order to rehabilitate the theory and concept of ideology one needs to do three things: (1) to move the theory of ideology from structure-centred approaches towards more agency-centred approaches; (2) to shift the emphasis from the function to the form and content of ideology and in this way to develop better research tools for the analysis of ideology; and (3) to apply these research tools to the study of the different articulations of ideology, among which the most important is the distinction between normative (official) and operative ideology (that is, ideology as an institutionalised narrative).

As we can see, both structuralism and poststructuralism operate with a similar concept of the social, giving an extremely strong, in the case of structuralism even a deterministic tone, in favour of structure over agency. Individual consciousness, autonomous will and an actor's rationality are not just completely negated, they are consciously expelled from the analysis. Structuralism and poststructuralism differ little in their rejection of the subject. Although this strategy of removing the subject from the analysis can produce neat and smooth historical and cultural essays, as in Baudrillard or Foucault, the analyses that exclude the role of agency certainly cannot properly explain the role ideologies play in social life. In their rejection of the subject and of ideology, poststructuralists treat this relationship as if it is circular and one-dimensional. The concept of ideology is rejected because it is perceived as a consciously employed device of manipulation of one class by another. On the other hand, individual autonomy is rejected because it is perceived as being completely historically determined and socially constructed. In other words, if there are no individual free wills, there can be no ideology, whereas if there is no ideology there can be no subject.

This line of thinking is problematic for at least two reasons. Firstly, as structuralists, and especially Althusser, show, there is no necessary relationship between the two; a theory of ideology is possible without a subject. Secondly, and more importantly for us, the agency and ideology can and do have many different forms of relationship. Ideologies certainly can and do include a level of manipulation, though this is not necessarily tied to class relations or to one social, economic or political order, and they can include any form of group membership (gender, nation, race, age, and so on) as well as being oriented to society as a whole. In fact every modern society, consciously or not, manipulates its young members through the education system, by forcing them to use textbooks with particular nationalistic interpretations of history and the social sciences. As Billig (1995) has nicely shown, 'banal nationalism' is a constant and often unnoticeable feature of everyday life – in the newspapers we read, in the television news we watch, through routine symbols and habits of language such as saluting the flag, expressing national pride, and so on.

Next, as we have learned from Weber (1968) individuals are attracted to a particular set of ideas, values and practices in at least four ways.[1] Firstly, this could be achieved through the form of instrumental rationality, meaning that individuals can be motivated in maximising their advantages that are in line with the teaching of the particular ideology.[2] The familiar and more extreme examples include support for the ideology that promotes ethnic cleansing or genocide that will result in acquiring houses, banks, land and other material goods from the expelled group, as was the case with the ideology of Nazism and the attitude of ordinary Germans to Jews in Nazi Germany (Goldhagen, 1996) or with the ideology of Serbian ethno-nationalism and Serbian popular perceptions of the Bosnian Muslims or Albanians in the recent wars on the territory of former Yugoslavia (Malešević, 2002).

Secondly, individual actors as well as groups can act on the basis of individual and group value-rationality, or what Boudon (1989) calls axiological rationality, meaning that individuals hold up to particular set of beliefs because they consider these values as promoting certain symbolic benefits for them. In Weber's words (1968, p. 25) actors believe 'in the value for its own sake of some ethical, aesthetic, religious, or other form of behaviour, independently of its prospects of success'. Hence, most citizens of the United States will support the values of liberal democracy without having broad knowledge, or even any knowledge at all, of the political theory of liberalism, predominantly because they associate these values with symbolic (and, of course, material) rewards generated within the framework of the American nation state. Similarly, Hezbollah suicide bombers and jihad warriors are motivated by the same belief in symbolic reward – all sins forgiven and a secure place in heaven.

Thirdly, ideologies can work through an emotional appeal where, in contrast with the first two ways, there is no clearly defined ideal of action. Individuals can act out of fear, hatred, love, the need for security, serenity or any other affect. This type of social action is more likely to take place in relatively short periods of time during or immediately after some dramatic social change (such as revolutions, wars, break-up of the state structure, natural disasters, and so on). Typical examples of this are the images associated with the close family and kinship ties ('our sons die for our motherland', 'our proletarian brothers', 'daughters of our nation', and so on).

Finally, actors can also maintain the traditional course of action, meaning that an individual will behave in accordance with habit and custom. As Weber (1968), Elias (1983) and Billig (1995) have convincingly argued, values, principles and ideas, that is ideologies, are very often reproduced and maintained almost exclusively through the habits of everyday life. By taking for granted symbols and practices around us, we maintain and reproduce many constructs of ideologies.

The answer to the question, 'why do individuals and groups accept and follow certain ideologies?' is not only to be found at the top of the social pyramid in structural manipulation (such as the 'fetishism of commodities' or logical structural patterns) or agency manipulation (the ruling class, the power-elite, the charismatic leader) but also at the bottom of the pyramid. The particular ideologies are well received by the majority of the population because they are successful in presenting themselves as being able to offer concrete material benefits, they appeal to particular interests and affects, they provide symbolic rewards, or they are simply part of traditional habitual action. The agency-centred theory of ideology needs to analyse in particular this relationship between the reception and receptors of ideology. The main questions here should be: what do ideologies offer to individuals? Why and how can individuals be motivated or persuaded to believe in particular ideologies? Why do individuals subscribe to one and not to another ideology? When, why and under which conditions is one articulation of an ideology preferred over another? Why are some interpreters ('articulators') more trusted than others?

It is important to emphasise here that this agency-centred theory of ideology does not neglect the role institutions of the state (which are often very important, if not crucial) play in the formation and dissemination of ideology, but unlike structuralism and poststructuralism it does not give primacy to institutions and structure. The institutions are no more than the means of and for individual and group action.

The next element is the need to shift the emphasis from the function to the form and content of ideology. As Lewins (1989, p. 680) and others have recognised, most approaches to ideology are focused on the functionality of ideology (examining what ideologies do), while there are very few approaches that are focused on the content of particular ideologies (examining what ideologies are, how they are composed, what their dominant themes are, and so on). Among the few theories that nominally concentrate on the content of ideology such as those of Pareto (1966) or Geertz (1964), there is very little serious analysis of ideology structure and content. Most of these approaches remain rather at the level of description or metaphor. In order to spot the similarities and differences between ideologies it is necessary to move our attention to the form and content of ideological narratives. The various action-oriented systems of beliefs, ideas and practices would hence be analysed and categorised by breaking them down into their constitutive elements in order to show similarities and differences between them. In this way we can secure a relatively simple but effective mechanism for the analysis of ideology. Thus, we need to identify and specify in detail conceptual segments of ideology. As a starting point I recommend seven such elements, analysis of which can help us to distinguish between the different ways any particular ideology may be structured. These include economy, politics, culture, the nation, dominant actors, type of language used and the depiction of principal counterideologies.[3]

First, ideology is related to the conceptual organisation of society. Therefore, the analysis would concentrate on statements and practices related to the four central categories that are vital for the functioning of any society:

(a) *economy* (production, distribution, consumption and exchange of goods and services);
(b) *politics* (political systems, dominant socio-political beliefs, power distribution and party structure);
(c) *culture* (articulation and dissemination of culture products, shared cultural values, stated directions of cultural policies and popular perceptions of culture); and
(d) *the nation* (what and who counts as a nation, the intensity and direction of nationalist feelings, the question of ethno-national homogeneity and the relationship between the nation and the state).

Second, every ideological narrative operates with a set of individual and group *actors*. The narratives depend on formulating and depicting the relationships between individuals and groups. They also portray social actors in different lights, attributing them different human or non-human characteristics. Hence, the analysis would look at how these individual and group actors have been described, what kinds of names, descriptions and images are associated with them, and so on.

Third, the research would also concentrate on the detailed analysis of the *language* used and other images present in the statements and practices. One should be able to assess the emotional, rational and other types of appeal in the particular ideological texts. This would also include the analysis of particular symbols, metaphors, the dynamics of their ambiguity and the intensity of their appeal.

Fourth, one needs also to study the way *counterideologies* are depicted and presented. This analysis would especially focus on the categorisation and descriptions of various counterideologies, from those that are perceived as directly threatening to those that are seen as potentially 'friendly'. One would in particular look here at the delegitimising strategies and tactics used.

This research strategy can be applied to a number of ideological texts regardless of their historical or geographical origins and location. The aim of such an analysis would be to single out similarities and differences between different ideological narratives, without treating any particular set of ideas and practices as being intrinsically privileged and hence accepting the criticism put forward by poststructuralists. In parallel with this activity, by identifying common features of ideologies, one would be in a position to make some theoretically interesting generalisations. In this way, if the model employed gives sufficient interpretation for the phenomena under study then it would achieve its main aim. It would provide the interpretation for the case studies under question and at the same time would demonstrate that the concept of ideology is still theoretically and methodologically viable. It would give an interpretation of ideology structure for particular societies or groups and would tell us at the same time something sociologically interesting about the concept of ideology.

However, in order not to reduce ideologies to party politics, worldviews, discourses or language games that have equal structural or ontological standings and thus lose the analytical strength of this concept, it is also necessary to distinguish between the two levels at which ideologies operate – that is normative (or official) and operative levels.[4]

Normative ideology refers to what Seliger would call 'fundamental principles which determine the final goals and the grand vistas in which they will be realised' (Seliger, 1976, p. 109). This form of ideology contains all the central pillars of any particular value system including views and ideas on the complete organisation and structure of past, present and future for the particular society. It spells out in a relatively clear and coherent way what relationships between individuals and groups are taking place and what ought to be, in order to change or preserve them. It gives a relatively consistent set of moral prescriptions, often based on a particular set of knowledge claims, and presents these prescriptions and claims as if addressing the entire humankind. This form of ideology is to be encountered in the works of influential philosophers, mystics, social scientists and prophets, in 'holy books' such as the Bible, Quran, Talmud or Vedas, in the constitutions of various nation states, in party programmes and manifestos, and so on.

Operative ideology is the form of ideology that one can encounter by analysing the features and patterns of everyday life in any given society. This type of ideology can consist of different conceptual elements and principles, some of which can serve to justify actual or potential social action. This is the form of ideology that penetrates and fills social life through institutional and non-institutional channels. It consists of commonly (but not universally) shared patterns of belief among the particular group of people in any given society. It is the way ideology functions and operates in the circumstances of daily routine. To identify and specify the form and content of this ideology, one has to analyse in detail such sources as the mass media, school textbooks, political rallies, political jokes, political and commercial advertisements, various pamphlets and leaflets, as well as political and commercial posters.

The relationship between the normative and the operative ideologies tends to be fairly complex and very much a matter of empirical evidence relating to individual case studies. The two can be composed of the same elements but they can also integrate entirely different ideas, values and practices. The cases of the Soviet Union and the Islamic Republic of Iran provide very good examples. As is evident from the analysis of their constitutions and numerous party resolutions (the Communist Party of the Soviet Union and the Islamic Republican Party) their normative ideologies were Marxism-Leninism and Shia Islam respectively. However, by analysing the patterns of their operative ideologies as they have been developed and have operated in the ritual practices, educational system, mass media and other social events and institutions, one could conclude that their operative ideologies were rather different – that is nationalist in the case of Iran (Ram, 2000) and imperialist and traditionalist (Lane, 1984) in the case of the Soviet Union.

In the study of dominant normative and operative ideologies of post-Second World War Yugoslavia and post-Cold War Serbia and Croatia I have tried to show how in each of the three cases normative and operative ideologies, while significantly different in terms of individual contents, were very similar, occasionally even identical, when analysing their form. While on the normative level dominant ideologies sharply differ, on the operative level they exhibit more similarities than differences. In all three cases it was differently artic-ulated nationalism that was identified as a dominant operative ideology: in the case of post-Second World War Yugoslavia the normative ideology was self-management socialism, whereas the dominant operative ideology was integral nationalist self-management socialism; in the case of post-Cold War Serbia the dominant normative ideology was reformed democratic socialism, while the dominant operative ideology was ethno-nationalist socialism; and in the case of post-Cold War Croatia the dominant normative ideology was ethno-nationalist Christian democracy, whereas the dominant operative ideology was Catholic ethno-nationalism (Malešević, 2002). A similar strategy, albeit in a more rudimentary form, was used also in comparing the central principles of ideologies of globalism and nationalism (Malešević, 1999).

These studies also demonstrated that the central research tool in the analysis of ideologies tends to be a comparative method, because by using this technique one is able to produce more generalised findings on the nature of ideology. The comparative analysis also allows examination of differently articulated ideologies without the need to make reference to the crude true–false criterion. The emphasis here is not any more on whether particular ideas, beliefs, values and practices are true or not, but rather on what they consist of, what kind of feelings and emotions they provoke, what kind of language they use, what they offer to their followers, what kind of action they provoke, and how they operate on normative and operative levels. In this way we will not focus rigidly and exclusively on the modes of production, on logical patterning or on discursive framing, as in structuralism and poststructuralism, in order to demonstrate that somebody else's views or actions are wrong and manipulative, but will rather focus on the form and contents of dif-ferently structured and articulated ideologies, in order to pinpoint their similarities and differences. The possible findings that this type of research could yield, such as that despite their contrasting and mutually exclusive normative ideologies Iran's and the United States' operative ideologies have much in common, would be at the same time politically provocative, theoretically interesting and sociolo-gically important.

By applying this analytic approach and comparative method we are in a position to overcome both unreflective and 'totalitarian' hard essentialism as well as the radical relativism and nihilism of poststructuralist critique. In other words, the theory and concept of ideology can be preserved by accepting and integrating some of the poststructuralist ideas, without the automatic incorporation of its relativist epistemology and its feeble research strategy.

CONCLUSION

In this chapter I have critically reviewed and analysed the main structuralist and poststructuralist approaches to the concept of ideology. I have tried to show that despite some positive criticism of poststructuralist approaches, such as their critique of the totalistic ambitions and hard essentialist methodology of structuralism, their complete rejection of the concept of the ideology is unfounded. Concepts such as 'discourse', 'language games', 'simulacras' or 'meta-narratives', recommended by poststructuralists in place of ideology, have been criticised as adding very little to the structuralist notion of ideology. It is thus argued that with the exception of clear and radical anti-scientism, poststructuralist approaches differ little from structuralism in their understanding of ideology. It is claimed that the concept and theory of ideology can be rehabilitated by removing it from its structuralist and Marxist emphasis on the truth, science and macrostructure. Instead, a new, more agency- and content-oriented theory of ideology has been proposed.

NOTES

1. Boudon (1989) recommends one more type of social action – situated rationality, which includes a different set of 'good reasons' that every individual can have in pursuing certain behaviour. Typical forms of situated rationality are rationality of position, where one's social, political, economic, cultural or any other position can determine the way one sees a particular situation, and dispositional rationality, where the knowledge that one has about a particular phenomenon can directly influence one's interpretation of it.

2. Other explanations that focus on instrumental rationality, such as rational choice theory (e.g. Downs, 1957, Heckathorn, 1998), explain ideologies with reference to individual actors' information costs. Hence actors subscribe to particular ideologies because of their lack of information and the costs of obtaining that information. In other words, if one intends to maximise one's net advantage, it is more rational and cheaper to follow the particular ideology than not to.

3. These seven categories by no means exhaust the possibilities. I have selected these particular categories simply because the great majority of all ideological narratives operate with them.

4. Similar distinction is also made in the works of Billig et al. (1988) and Freeden (1996). Billig distinguishes between intellectual and lived ideology, while Freeden talks about elitist and popular ideologies.

REFERENCES

Althusser, L. (1994) 'Ideology and Ideological State Apparatuses (Notes towards an Investigation)', in Žižek, S. (ed.) *Mapping Ideology* (London: Verso).

Barrett, M. (1991) *The Politics of Truth: From Marx to Foucault* (Cambridge: Polity).

Barthes, R. (1972) *Mythologies* (London: Cape).

Baudrillard, J. (1988) *Simulacra and Simulations* (Cambridge: Polity Press).

Beck, U. (1991) *Risk Society* (Cambridge: Polity Press).

Bevir, M. (1999) 'Foucault and Critique: Deploying Agency against Autonomy', *Political Theory*, vol. 27, no. 1, pp. 65–84.

Billig, M. (1995) *Banal Nationalism* (London: Sage).

Billig, M. *et al.* (1988) *Ideological Dilemmas: A Social Psychology of Everyday Thinking* (London: Sage).

Boudon, R. (1989) *The Analysis of Ideology* (Cambridge: Polity Press).

Downs, A. (1957) *An Economic Theory of Democracy* (New York: Harper and Row).

Elias, N. (1983) *The Court Society* (Oxford: Blackwell).

Foucault, M. (1977) *Discipline and Punish: the Birth of the Prison* (London: Allen Lane).

Foucault, M. (1980) 'Truth and Power', in Gordon, C. (ed.) *Michael Foucault, Power/Knowledge* (Brighton: Harvester Press).

Fox, N. (1998) 'Foucault, Foucauldians and Sociology', *British Journal of Sociology*, vol. 49, no. 3, pp. 415–433.

Freeden, M. (1996) *Ideologies and Political Theory: A Conceptual Approach* (Oxford: Clarendon Press).

Geertz, C. (1964) 'Ideology as a Cultural System', in Apter, D. (ed.) *Ideology and Discontent* (New York: Free Press).

Giddens, A. (1987) 'Structuralism, Post-Structuralism and the Production of Culture', in Giddens, A. and Turner, J. (eds) *Social Theory Today* (Cambridge: Polity).

Giddens, A. (1991) *Modernity and Self-Identity: Self and Society in the Late Modern Age* (Cambridge: Polity).

Giddens, A. (1992) *The Transformation of Intimacy: Sexuality, Love and Eroticism in Modern Societies* (Cambridge: Polity).

Goldhagen, D. (1996) *Hitler's Willing Executioners: Ordinary Germans and the Holocaust* (New York: Knopf).

Gouldner, A. (1970) *The Coming Crisis of Western Sociology* (New York: Basic Books).

Habermas, J. (1987) *The Philosophical Discourse of Modernity* (Cambridge: MIT Press).

Heckathorn, D. (1998) 'Collective Action, Social Dilemmas, and Ideology', *Rationality and Society*, vol. 10, no. 4, pp. 451–480.

Laclau, E. and Mouffe, C. (1985) *Hegemony and Socialist Strategy* (London: Verso).

Lane, C. (1984) 'Legitimacy and Power in the Soviet Union Through Socialist Ritual', *British Journal of Political Science*, vol.14, no. 1, pp. 207–217.

Larrain, J. (1994) 'The Postmodern Critique of Ideology', *The Sociological Review*, vol. 42, no. 2, pp. 289–314.

Lévi-Strauss, C. (1975) *The Raw and the Cooked* (New York: Harper and Row).

Lewins, F. (1989) 'Recasting the Concept of Ideology: A Content Approach', *British Journal of Sociology*, vol. 40, no. 4, pp. 678–693.

Lyotard, F. (1984) *The Postmodern Condition: A Report on Knowledge* (Manchester: Manchester University Press).

Malešević, S. (1999) 'Globalism and Nationalism: Which One is Bad?', *Development in Practice*, vol. 9, no. 5, pp. 579–583.

Malešević, S. (2002) *Ideology, Legitimacy and the New State: Yugoslavia, Serbia and Croatia* (London: Frank Cass).

Malinowski, B. (1926) *Myth in Primitive Psychology* (Westport: Negro Universities Press).

Marcuse, H. (1971) *One-Dimensional Man: Studies in the Ideology of Advanced Industrial Society* (Boston: Beacon Press).

Pareto, V. (1966) *Sociological Writings* (Oxford: Basil Blackwell).

Parsons, T. (1991) 'A Tentative Outline of American Values', in Robertson, R. and Turner, B.S. (eds) *Talcot Parsons – Theorist of Modernity* (London: Sage).

Ram, H. (2000) 'The Immemorial Iranian Nation? School Textbooks and Historical Memory in Post-revolutionary Iran', *Nations and Nationalism*, vol. 6, no. 1, pp. 67–90.

Sartori, G. (1969) 'Politics, Ideology and Belief Systems', *American Political Science Review*, vol. 63, no.1, pp. 398–411.

Seliger, M. (1976) *Ideology and Politics* (London: Allen and Unwin).

Shils, E. (1968) 'The Concept and Function of Ideology', *International Encyclopaedia of the Social Sciences*, vol. 7, pp. 66–76.

Taylor, C. (1984) 'Foucault on Freedom and Truth', *Political Theory*, vol. 12, no. 2, pp. 152–183.

Weber, M. (1968) *Economy and Society, I–II* (New York: Bedminster Press).

6　The Dialectics of the Real

Diana Coole

Is there ideology after poststructuralism? The question is certainly a provocative one, but what does it mean? It implies that there is something wrong with ideology, a problem for which poststructuralism is at least in part responsible. Yet its wounds are perhaps not terminal: it still commands our affections sufficiently to summon reappraisal. What can this reappraisal entail, coming *after* poststructuralism? Are we to return to a concept which once appeared obsolete but whose loss we now mourn, rediscovering riches to which poststructuralism perhaps did an injustice? Are we to rehearse, maybe now with greater clarity, the reasons we abandoned such a troubled term in the first place? Or is this an invitation to explore some possible synthesis or *rapprochement*, whereby ideology might now be reborn but inflected through poststructuralist perspectives? It seems to me that the question could plausibly be interpreted in any of these ways: as a nostalgic revisiting of the past; as a more precise engagement in current debates, or as a call for experiments towards the future. Accordingly I will try to address all three.

If poststructuralist sympathies have challenged the very idea of ideology, why should we wish to rescue or reinvigorate it? Does this desire not imply some discomfort with the poststructuralist project too; a lacuna we hope some reconstituted understanding of ideology might overcome? To put it rather schematically: it seems to me that this desire and discomfort arise from *political* concerns and from a now widespread sense that the relativisms and multiplicities vaunted by poststructuralism cannot deliver the sort of critical or reconstructive politics once anticipated. It is true that they invoke a sort of creative, experimental and aleatory whirlwind that summons a break with the continuum of history in the name of a new people and a deterritorialised politics (Deleuze and Guattari, 1994). The insistence on openness does suggest an enduringly critical attitude inasmuch as democracy, justice, communism are always to come (*à-venir*) – not in the future but as the spectres that haunt every present by preventing its closure. Held at a distance via an ethic of responsibility to the other, they defy the thermidor which has historically followed every revolt and the authoritarianism inherent in every rational (and irrational) plan for a free society.[1] What seems to be missing nevertheless is a process of critical engagement in what might once have been called the real world. For there is little concrete analysis of socio-economic or state structures in the contemporary social formation and therefore little sense of how to change them.[2] If poststructuralism has ethical and utopian credentials,[3] it thus lacks the determinate negations which might endow them with efficacy. As such, poststructuralism might itself be designated ideological by those who follow the early Marx in equating ideology with idealist philosophies that alter consciousness without changing the material world.[4]

It is in this context that many who still associate themselves with a radical (leftist) political agenda have been reluctant to abandon the idea, difficult as it now is to state with the requisite philosophical and deconstructive rigour, that powerful groups or institutions in society rely upon a variety of mechanisms which reproduce the conditions of their privilege, where these include something that is usefully labelled ideological. Whether ideology is understood here in the narrower sense of ideas that sustain particular privileges, or in a broader sense as the taken-for-granted horizons of a culture, a search for some more robust way of distinguishing between conservative and critical discourses than poststructuralism apparently offers probably explains the enduring attractiveness of some concept of ideology. The relating of these discourses to the force field of the present similarly explains the appeal of ideology critique. Certain questions then follow. First, can ideology's *political* utility be rescued without ignoring the *epistemological* challenges poststructuralists pose? And second, is there an alternative to widespread suggestions that ideology has either ended or is (now) sufficiently ubiquitous to be unrecognisable, unavoidable and therefore essentially meaningless? I think it is important to keep these two questions at least analytically distinct since the first involves the very idea of ideology, which interests philosophers, while the second is more concerned with its sociological relevance (in this latter case ideology might be a coherent concept but one whose historical relevance has atrophied).

I will not have space in this chapter to explore the second question, except to note that it cannot be resolved other than by a critical analysis of recent global developments. I will focus rather on some of the criticisms poststructuralists have made of the very idea of ideology. But I will then argue that it was precisely the (dialectical) connection between philosophy and sociological analysis, which discourses concerned with ideology once insisted upon, that is missing from poststructuralism and the reason for a continuing enchantment with ideology.

THE CASE AGAINST IDEOLOGY

Much of the poststructuralist case against ideology hinges on its implication in the sort of binary oppositions its exponents famously deconstruct. As a result, ideology is thrown under suspicion of being metaphysical and more specifically, of relying upon the Enlightenment's rationalist and subjectivist foundations. In this context anxieties about ideology have fused with more general epistemological and ontological concerns related to the philosophical foundations Descartes and Kant developed at the beginning of modernity. For both these thinkers, knowledge entailed the imposition of methodological or categorial classifications on the natural world. As such, rationality was the provenance of a knowing subject who brought order to the objective domain. Hegelian dialectics was developed as a way of thinking a more reciprocal, mediated relation between subject and object, humanity and nature, whereby all these terms as well as their relationships are produced historically. It is therefore ironic that more explicit attacks on ideology have tended to be inflected through poststructuralists' antipathy towards Marxism. For this antipathy draws in turn on the rejection of Hegelian dialectics which is characteristic of most poststructuralists.

As a result of these philosophical antagonisms, it then appears that hostility towards ideology is but one aspect of a more general incredulity towards each of modernity's two major meta-narratives – the liberal-emancipatory one associated with Kant and the speculative one derived from Hegel[5] – both of which are accused of a philosophically misguided and politically dangerous rationalism. It is on this fundamental level that its critique has then to be addressed. Here the debate broadly translates into support for Nietzsche against *both* Descartes/Kant *and* Hegel/Marx. I suggest that the rather different cases against these two targets have tended in fact to become elided, leading to an unwarranted dismissal of the dialectical approach, which was itself developed as a way of overcoming many of the oppositions and difficulties poststructuralists now cite and which dialecticians themselves identified with

Descartes and Kant. It is then by returning to a more sympathetic understanding of dialectics as a critical methodology – albeit one which looks less different from genealogy than poststructuralists would have us believe – that a politically useful and epistemologically tenable sense of ideology might be regained. In other words, I am arguing that the fate of ideology hangs on a reappraisal of dialectics, since the two are inseparable. Outside of this connection ideology looks vulnerable to accusations of a rather crude form of rationalism, such as poststructuralists often level.

In order to consider more carefully the broad oppositions and antagonisms so far alluded to, it will be useful to start with the confrontation between post-Nietzscheans and Hegel/Marx: one that can in turn be usefully transcribed, I suggest, into affirmation versus negation. It is in these terms that the significant difference between poststructuralist (and vitalist) and dialectical politics comes into relief, although one can also discern here more *critical* continuity than is generally acknowledged. Here is a brief philosophical excursus in support of such transpositions and claims.

In what Habermas has categorised as critical discourses of modernity, the figure of the negative is indicative of a radical, emancipatory politics. Yet poststructuralists often voice considerable hostility towards the negative. A good place to begin in understanding why, is Deleuze's reading of Nietzsche. Deleuze's 1962 *Nietzsche and Philosophy* was immensely influential among poststructuralists and their own reception of Nietzsche as an alternative to Marx. Deleuze makes much of the fact that in his *Genealogy of Morality*, Nietzsche had attacked the *ressentiment* of the slave mentality as a simply reactive, life-denying and thus nihilistic orientation. It was portrayed as merely negative. For unlike the nobles who affirm life in its joyous excess, the *plebs* identify themselves solely through opposition. They say no to everything that is other and establish their identity only as not being masters. Against the masters' celebrations, which are beyond good and evil, the slaves oppose ascetic morality and enervating bad conscience. Whereas for Hegel and Marx the master–slave dialectic had been politically explosive and historically fecund, with the slave-proletarians negating master-capitalist domination in order to set humanity free, Nietzsche identified no progressive political interaction between them. Instead he appeared to look beyond the oppositional form itself and towards a new economy of life. Here a ferment of creative-destruction occurs and differential intensities are celebrated without desire for synthesis or negation. The young Deleuze interpreted all this in Manichean terms. 'Nietzsche's "yes" is opposed to the dialectical "no"; affirmation to dialectical negation; difference to dialectical contradiction; joy, enjoyment, to dialectical labour; lightness, dance, to dialectical responsibilities' (Deleuze, 1983, p. 9).

More ontologically, Deleuze derived from the play of differential intensities that describe the dynamics of Nietzsche's will to power, a process of becoming through differenciation that is more positive and multiplicitous than the contradictions and negations described by dialectics. In other words, he appeals to a different rhythm of generativity than the labour of the negative described by dialectics: one where there is a productive difference without opposition or negation. Dialectic, he would go on to write in *Difference and Repetition*, 'thrives on oppositions because it is unaware of far more subtle and subterranean differential mechanisms: topographical displacements, typographical mechanisms' (Deleuze, 1983, p. 158). Beneath the platitude of the negative, he insists, there lies the world of 'disparateness' (Deleuze, 1994, p. 266). Change is not then engendered by contradiction and negation but through a repetition of singularities whose small divergencies produce unexpected novelty and facilitate unpredictable experimentation. From this perspective dialectics, with its choreography of determinate negations, binary-looking contradictions and syntheses, remains too close to logical and grammatical forms with their emphasis on identity. It seems to reduce non-identity and difference to reason. It is too lawful. 'There is no synthesis, mediation or reconciliation in difference', Deleuze contends, 'but rather a stubborn differenciation' (Deleuze, 1994, p. 202f.). It was this wild, positive generativity that Nietzsche had termed will to power. He had anticipated its exemplification in a Dionysian revaluation of all values whose participants would say yes to life, where life is itself described *as* will to power. As far as politics is concerned, Deleuze concludes that history progresses not via negation, but 'by deciding problems and affirming differences'. 'Only the shadows of history live by negation: the good enter into it with all the power of a posited differential or a difference affirmed' (Deleuze, 1994, p. 268). Although Deleuze explicitly opposes positivity and affirmation to dialectical negativity in his work, it is nevertheless evident that Nietzschean generativity does fulfil a critical, negativist role inasmuch as it challenges positive, reified forms (like asceticism, religious or egalitarian ideologies, stultified herd-consciousness, the Oedipalised unconscious) which are uniformly nihilistic in denying life. It is this Nietzschean-inspired antipathy towards the negative in its dialectical sense, coupled with the generalised hostility to reified structures it shares with dialectics, that can subsequently be discerned among most poststructuralist and postmodern thinkers.

The rejection of the negative here is more or less synonymous with an attack on Hegelian dialectics, where difference seems merely to enhance identity; determinate negation is implicated in what it opposes and the negation of the negation looks like an overcoming of alterity in a positive lifting up (*relève*). It is the latter which yields what looks like a rationalistic meta-narrative: a process that will finally transcend difference, non-identity, particularity. It has no responsibility to the Other (to Life, to the nonrational fulminations of the heterogeneous, the multiple, the material) apart from its assimilation into rational knowledge and reduction, thereby, to the Same. The itinerary trodden by the negative is totalising (read total-itarian) as well as teleological. According to this reading of dialectics, negativity succumbs to positivism, difference to identity, diversity to the gulag. It is little different, after all, from the Cartesian ration-alism that results in the domination of nature or the Kantian categorical imperative whose outcome is Terror.[6] Marxism generally, and its conception of ideology in particular, are then implicated in this critique, where ideology looks like a temporary failure of reason to reach its goals of identity and truth and where the overcoming of ideology means using reason to put Reason back on course.

It is this kind of attack on dialectics that also drives Derrida's sense of *différance*, whose play is explicitly opposed to Hegelianism. Because opposition and rational argument would merely verify the rationalising progress of the dialectic, it is necessary instead to operate the 'radical displacement' that is attributed to *différance* (Derrida, 1982, p. 14). If *différance* could be defined, Derrida explains, it 'would be precisely the limit, the interruption, the destruction of the Hegelian *relève* [*aufhebung*] wherever *it operates*' (Derrida, 1981, p. 40). Deconstructive practices are then summoned precisely to dislocate the synthetic process; to disrupt temporal succession and a phenomenology of meaning by deferral and the incision of intervals that rupture any possible unity. Although Derrida's appeal to Saussurean linguistics, where there are only differences without positive terms, looks more negative than does Deleuzean difference (and Deleuze himself criticises Saussure for presenting differences as negative rather than affirmative and productive (Deleuze, 1994,

p. 204f.)), the aim is still nevertheless to invoke a generativity that is heterogeneous and nonlogical, affirmative in the sense of being playful, creative, productive. Synthetic becoming is always deferred, scattered by undecidables. Instead of antithesis and synthesis there is inversion and subversion. The spacing that produces effects and interrupts all identity, Derrida writes, 'carries the meaning of a productive, positive, generative force' (Derrida, 1981, p. 106f.). *Différance* does not work through mediation or contradiction but is the differentiating process itself.

Derrida gives the description a normative gloss by calling on us to affirm such *différance* by dance and laughter without nostalgia (for identity or totality): an affirmation which he designates 'foreign to all dialectics' (Derrida, 1982, p. 27). Against dialectical totalising, he insists, dissemination marks an irreducible and generative multiplicity where closure or totality are always rendered impossible. Subsequently this procedure is used to deconstruct both Hegel's system (in *Glas*) and Marx's allegedly totalising thought (in *Specters*). In the latter case, Derrida's reading is designed precisely to subvert what he sees as a faulty ontology in Marx, whereby communism is seen as an absence to be brought into presence, made real. His aim is to rescue Marx from a series of oppositions, centred on presence/absence, reality/appearance, that for Derrida spook his radicalism.

This sense of an affirmative, non-totalising productivity is then indicative of most poststructuralisms (think of Lyotard's experimental war on totality or Foucault's assault on negative accounts of power as opposed to its heterogeneous, constitutive flows). Broadly it signifies the possibility of a surprise, an event, a rupture with the past which is antithetical to the unfolding logic of dialectics; an aleatory process rather than the immanent logic and determinations of the dialectic.

This affirmation must nevertheless be understood in a far more complex way than simply as one side of a positive–negative opposition. First there is the affirmative celebration of (quasi-)ontological flux, contingency, heterogeneity, which resist the oppositional figure itself as too rationalistic, logical, lawful. Poststructuralist writing is designed to exemplify these qualities to a greater or lesser extent, as opposed to the demystification which ideology critique practises. A politics modelled on this process would necessarily remain unpredictable, with 'progress' having nothing to do with the discovery of truth. If congealed institutions and structures of privilege provoke censure, then the particular resistances they incite, like the experiments which might transfigure them, remain immune to theoretical prophecy. They thereby elude the rationalist projects of the past (associated with the Enlightenment and implicating its progressive as well as its conservative ideological movements in authoritarianism), but do they also lose transformative efficacy?

A second and more specific argument concerns the way post-structuralists oppose discourse to ideology in a way that summons their respective positive and negative affinities rather differently. In their typical Foucaultian version, discourses are presented as positive *qua* productive; that is, as *constitutive* of truth, as opposed to ideology's negative function of obscuring it. (In the half-way house of the Althusserian version, ideology itself becomes productive, in particular of subjectivity.) It will be necessary to return to this argument shortly but in this context it serves to highlight the way ideology is seen as negative. Like the political and juridical understanding of power which Foucault contests, it focuses only on forces of denial and suppression. Ideology thus looks merely negative inasmuch as it is something that denies and mystifies, hides and obscures; it is associated with lack, false consciousness and error. It is social theories predicated on this negativist approach that have fallen victim to the more affirmative rendition, where affirmation now means producing rather than blocking. Accordingly ideology is no longer opposed to *science* (as false consciousness versus truth) but on the one hand to *philosophy* (as creative and productive, in a good sense)[7] and on the other, to *discourse* (as constitutive and productive but in a power-suffused sense). Unlike ideology, discourse carries no hope of overcoming the power-relations it involves; at best one discursive regime would be replaced by another (in this sense such regimes are more like descriptive senses of ideological horizons). Ideology's negative aspects of appearance, error and distortion are perceived as meaningful only in the binary context of their antitheses: reality, rationality, Truth. It is its dependence on the latter that is seen as the rationalist flaw in Marxist theories of ideology: a flaw derived from an uncritical acceptance of certain Enlightenment presuppositions concerning subjectivity, objectivity and humanism. Ironically, Marx's problem here was that he was not critical enough. It looks as if he committed the grave error of assuming a pre-discursive reality against which knowledge is judged.

Inasmuch as Marx would look like a *positivist* here, such positivism must, finally, be distinguished from the affirmation discussed above. For dialectical thinkers, negative thinking involves criticism of the given in terms of what it is not but has the potential to become. This is opposed by them to positivism, which covers a raft of approaches from logical positivism to empiricism and is accused of a one-dimensional and uncritical presentation of the given.[8] Such thinking is of course at odds with the affirmation which, if it eschews the critical negativity of determinate negation, also presents the given as highly dynamic and immune to representation. But it is also quite at odds with anything except the crudest Marxism.

In this section I have tried to unpack some of the poststructuralist arguments against the concept of ideology, showing how it is implicated in broader targets whose common flaw is their rationalism. I have suggested that a helpful way of understanding these polemics is to cast them in a complex field of positive versus negative permutations. In the next section I will explain how, in so far as ideology is understood in this negative way, it must however be grasped in terms of Marx's more extensive philosophy of negativity and that from this perspective, poststructuralism and Marxism have more in common than the former acknowledges. The crucial issue here seems to be the senses and relationships attributed to the real and the true and these must also be addressed more explicitly, via a return to Foucault.

PHILOSOPHIES IN THE NEGATIVE

If ideology is negative for Marx inasmuch as it implies a deficit of reason, this understanding has nevertheless to be understood in the context of his more general philosophy of negativity, derived from Hegel and centring on defining aspects of historical materialism as a dialectical methodology. According to this approach, no social or symbolic form is natural or absolute because every identity results from a process of negation. There is a continuous mediation of identity and difference, subject and object, which also engenders them. Everything is in the process of becoming. Although there is a certain inertia and interest in history that works to sustain the status quo and thus prevent change (specifically, for Marx, class interests) the present, according to dialectical thinking, inevitably finds itself succumbing to oppositional forces it cannot finally control or suppress. Historical materialism tries then to discern this interplay between positive and negative – between stabilising, reactionary forces and progressive, transformative ones – at any historical moment. Typically, the tension they generate takes place between (dynamic) forces of production and (reifying) social relations of production.

Ideology is one component of this drama because, as Marx makes clear where he renders it synonymous with German Idealism, it refers to those ideas that make the present look unassailable or unsurpassable. In this sense it is one of the forces that support the positive – that is, what has presence, privilege and power under existing arrangements. Ideology critique, on the other hand, involves a practising of negativity: a critical assault on the illusion that things can resist change and are not in-process or that they benefit all universally rather than privileging particular groups. The aim of such ideological demystification is to set history in motion once more, by galvanising those who suffer the injustices of the present as their fate. Of course, for Marx (and Hegel) it is not just the resumption of process per se that is important, but the fact that process means progress: towards more universal forms that will transcend the partiality and errors, the scarcity and exploitation, of the past. History's blockages are to be negated by a variety of critical interventions that must, to be effective, culminate in a material praxis which instantiates a culturally richer, more rational and synthetic, collective life. Here the rational involves a constellation of senses: not only a clearer knowledge of history's trajectories which guides action (praxis) and production organised on a rational basis (planning) but also, an integration of the particular and the universal. To the extent that all this looks like a recipe for a closed totality, teleologically anticipated as history's true culmination, poststructuralist anxiety seems entirely warranted. But inasmuch as dialectical wholes resonate with diverse perspectives, history's contingency is acknowledged and reason involves critically defensible social arrangements; a dialectical methodology avoids these concerns.

In fact, the sort of Nietzschean-inspired affirmation or genealogy embraced by many poststructuralists is quite consonant with Marx's negativity here, as a political project. For its aim is also to resist and transgress reified and immobile forms and to release the forces that would subvert them (an ambition helped in the West, as a variety of thinkers from Kristeva to Foucault concede, by the demise of two millennia of Christianity). Of course the ontology and rhythms underpinning the poststructuralist version are quite at odds with dialectical negativity. But the basic *political* opposition between what is instituted and static (boundaries and limits as well as structures and stratifications) and irruptions which will destabilise it, is a shared one. In both cases, negative forces are immanent and theory both clears spaces for and helps constitute the agencies which will set them in motion. Hegelianism/Marxism as well as poststructuralism can all then be classified as philosophies of negativity inasmuch as they pursue a politics that opposes the positivity of the given (for example the misrepresentations and illusions of subjectivity as well as of capital). In all cases, some disruptive and irrepressible generativity is invoked in order to destabilise congealed institutions and immobile powers. If ideology designates those performative or discursive acts that sustain closure by immunising the positive against change, then something like it is operative in all these approaches.

It is nonetheless necessary to distinguish here between a pejorative, critical sense of ideology and a more neutral definition of discursive regimes which merely, monotonously, follow one another. It is the former that lends political bite, yet it is precisely this point, concerning the criterion of the pejorative (against what is it being measured to yield this negative judgement?), that is most contentious. Marxian senses of ideology look problematic inasmuch as they seem to rely on a meta-narrative whereby overcoming illusions and obfuscations would return History to its correct path, rather than simply opening it to the agonistic play of power and resistance. This is where ideology looks as if it relies upon a metaphysical conception of truth. At the same time, appeals to a truth against which ideological falsity is measured invoke more general concerns about epistemology and representation, where evocations of the real as true ring poststructuralist alarm bells. This then brings me to the next part of my argument, concerning dialectical senses of the true and the real.

THE TRUE AND THE REAL

I will start here with Foucault, because he is so explicit on this issue. Foucault gives three reasons for finding the notion of ideology 'difficult' (though not impossible, note: he only warns us against using it 'without circumspection'). His first is the following: 'like it or not, it always stands in virtual opposition to something else which is supposed to count as truth'. In place of this impossible ideological distinction he proffers genealogy: 'seeing historically how effects of truth are produced within discourses which in themselves are neither true nor false'. Foucault then goes on to offer two additional concerns about the notion of ideology: it refers – 'I think necessarily' – to the subject and it is epiphenomenal, that is, relative to a material determinant ('etc.') (Foucault, 1972, p. 118). In sum, Foucault condemns ideology owing to its alleged dependence on three oppositions: truth/error; subject/object; base/superstructure. Its difficulties are thus coexistent with Marxism in its entirety. But is Foucault's rendition of ideology fair and does he offer us compelling grounds for rejecting it? This hinges on the question of whether it *necessarily* relies on the trio of oppositions he elicits.

I will begin with a rather general point here. It would be easy in light of poststructuralist attacks to forget that dialectical thinkers never do posit binary oppositions as such and certainly not in any metaphysical or ontological way. If oppositions are recognised, these are always in a dialectical process of reciprocity that is highly dynamic, unstable and productive of the opposing terms themselves. If they harden into contradictions, then this is a sign that their internal relationship has been foreclosed and a more explosive negation is going to be needed before that relationship can resume.

It is with this in mind that the first opposition, between truth and error, is approached. This is the one most explicitly associated with ideology and the one about which I will therefore have most to say here, especially since it tends to subsume the other two. In elaborating on his antipathy towards the category of truth, Foucault rejects any sense in which it lies undefiled behind power, waiting as a reward for liberation. Truth is engendered within 'régimes of truth' which are not, he insists, 'merely ideological or superstructural', but conditions of possibility for economic forms like capitalism. The essential political task, he concludes, does not lie in criticising ideological contents or acquiring a correct ideology. Much less – as in fact Marx had explicitly noted – can it be a case of changing consciousness in isolation from its political and economic supports. For Foucault politics is rather about engaging with the discursive régimes that produce truth. ('The political question ... is not error, illusion, alienated consciousness or ideology; it is truth itself' (Foucault, 1972, p. 133)). Such discursive regimes, it might be inferred, operate more like will to power than ideology in that they are internally generative of a range of symbolic, material and institutional effects. This is perhaps what Foucault has in mind in his last caveat, where ideology is rejected as epiphenomenal, superstructural. For here it sometimes looks like an effect of prior, non-discursive, economic causes. His concern echoes Nietzsche's condemnation of cause/effect relations as entailing a doer behind the deed, as opposed to will to power's internal generativity. From this perspective it makes no sense to condemn discourse as such, as a Marxist might describe all ideology in pejorative (negative) terms. One can only attempt to shift particular discursive configurations, where there is sufficient room for manoeuvre, and replace them with others.

As far as truth and error are concerned, for dialectical thinkers their relationship is neither causal nor simply oppositional. Truth evolves out of error: not via acts of discovery, but through an ongoing process whereby partial truths are confronted by their limits. It is a product of intersubjective and existential interactions over time. Ideology in this context is erroneous because it blocks further explorations and interrogations, thus freezing truths which become erroneous as they move out of kilter with a world in process.

Where I think the true/false opposition becomes most resonant for poststructuralists is, however, where it is treated as more or less synonymous with the distinction between reality and appearance. This distinction is important to them inasmuch as they are captivated by Nietzsche's claim that metaphysics presents the real as the true in order to dismiss or condemn appearances as false, because they are shifting and contingent. Dialectical thinkers seem to echo this division and its hierarchy when they contend that the real becomes true when it is sufficiently mediated (as opposed to the illusion of immediacy borne by *mere* appearances). It is nevertheless important, I want to insist, that these dialectical and Nietzschean arguments are kept distinct because they are in fact quite different. Poststructuralist attacks on ideology's opposition between true (reality) and false (appearances) tend to get inflected, however, through Nietzsche's attack on Kant and this then distorts their readings of Marx. In other words, this is where the arguments relative to modernity's two meta-narratives become misleadingly conflated.

Nietzsche had implicated Kant, among others, in the metaphysical distinction between reality and appearance. Kantian epistemology is also, of course, one of the main targets of poststructuralist critiques of the Enlightenment. So what has happened, I am suggesting, is that dialectics gets caught up in the general attack on Enlightenment rationalism. Although Marx is certainly vulnerable to aspects of this, the Nietzschean-inspired reading both distorts the notion of reality which dialectics intends and, paradoxically if implicitly, attributes

124 Ideology After Poststructuralism

to Marx the very Kantian dualism which Hegelian dialectics was intended to overcome. How does this reversal work?

In his *Critique of Pure Reason*, Kant had famously tried to overcome scepticism via his Copernican Revolution. The aim here was to sidestep the dilemma which seems to occur whenever knowledge claims rely upon accessing the thing in itself. The result, he shows, is either dogmatism or scepticism, since there is no possibility of the sort of verification that could satisfy criteria of critical reason. Kant accordingly argues that we must forget about knowing the thing in itself since any knowledge we could conceivably have is already structured by the forms which the senses and the categories of the understanding impose upon the world. This is indeed the precondition of our knowing it at all. He thus made a famous distinction between noumena, which are irremediably off limits, and phenomena, which are the representations we do know since they result from subjective faculties. Although Kant's efforts to sustain the distinction got him into difficulties,[9] the impossibility of knowing the in itself has been widely accepted ever since. (This has not however caused any practical difficulty since Kant offered a realist, correspondence theory of truth when it came to phenomena: since we structure their appearances, we know them indubitably.)

Hegel accepted these epistemological limits when he acknowledged that the immediacy with which his books often begin is only an origin under erasure, since anything we can say, know or even perceive is already mediated. Identifying anything relies on a process of differentiation and determinate negation. But the aim of dialectics was precisely to overcome the dualism of an inert, unknowable noumenal other (or for that matter an equally inert, fully known phenomenal immediacy), and an ahistorical subjectivity. Dialectical becoming is a production of, as well as a reciprocity between, subject and object. In this sense Hegelian reality is never some noumenal immediacy underlying phenomena but is closer to what the young Marx's existentialist followers called existence: that place where practical and cognitive interventions, material and ideal forces, meet in a highly dynamic way. It is in the phenomenal realm that meaning appears, and references to 'mere' appearances are never intended to imply that they are opposed to the thing in itself. If this phenomenal reality becomes rational – actual – this is only through a process of mediations whereby the web of relations that support every provisional identity as complex and in process is articulated over time.

Nietzsche's attack on Kantian metaphysics also challenged the idea of the thing in itself underlying appearances, but on quite different grounds. Kantianism was for Nietzsche only part of a nihilistic and ascetic metaphysics that opposes a true, unchanging higher world to the shifting phenomena of Life in order to denigrate the latter. Unlike Hegel he does not offer a phenomenology of meaning whereby appearances yield up their partial truths until the real becomes rational; rather, appearances remain unmediated, a shifting configuration of perspectives that coagulate and disintegrate through a combination of random and colonising moves (hence the will to power, or capillary power, that the genealogist describes). Nietzsche is no more an empiricist of the phenomenal than are Hegel and Marx, because for him appearances are always veils, masks, but there is no sense of an underlying truth that might disclose or expose them.

Now, when poststructuralists read the Nietzschean/Foucaultian appeal to genealogy, this rejection of the in itself becomes generalised, it seems to me, to a broad proscription on any claims that look as if they appeal to the real, since this is now understood as a metaphysical gesture towards the noumenal (and following Lacan, this is seductively labelled the impossible Real). It now looks, then, as if the Marxist sense of ideology relies on an illegitimate Kantian distinction between Truth and appearances. Worse, it is even pre-critical in claiming access to Reality, to Truth, in itself (an hallucinatory metaphysics of transcendental realism as Kant would have put it). I am not quite claiming that these unwarranted elisions are explicitly made, but I am suggesting that they tend to operate implicitly because of the route by which many of poststructuralism's admirers have taken up its critiques of Marxism and its sense of ideology.

As far as dialectics is concerned, it would be entirely illegitimate to claim that it seeks either unmediated access to immediacy or a correspondence theory of truth. But inflected through neo-Nietzscheanisms, ideology does begin to look like a naïve claim to knowledge of the social formation purged of false consciousness and distortion. As such, it looks suspiciously like a version of the will to truth and vulnerable to postmodern concerns about representation. Furthermore, it seems to be part of the modern, rationalist fantasy of an end to chaos and conflict, power and politics, where the overcoming of ideology that motivates ideology critique would mean redemption, harmony, transparency, consensus. This suspicion could be expressed in quite other terms politically – for example as Rousseau versus Machiavelli – and it is also fed by post-structuralist disquiet towards Habermas's ideal speech situation. But it implicates ideology in the whole Nietzschean distrust of Western metaphysics as life-denying and therefore nihilistic.

Poststructuralist concerns about appeals to the real as the true are further reinforced by more traditional liberal anxieties. One has only to think here of Isaiah Berlin's identification of positive liberty with a dangerous authoritarianism he identifies with Rousseau and Stalinism, whereby an elite would claim knowledge of an authentic freedom unavailable to the mystified masses as a way of legitimis-ing its own rule (Berlin, 1969). Or one might recall the concerns that Lukes' (1974) third dimension of power provoked in its appeal to the proletariat's 'real' but veiled interests, which was again accused of dangerously elitist or paternalist implications.[10] Liberal fears of authoritarianism and poststructuralist anxieties about totalitarian-ism converge here. Where they differ, of course, is in liberals' belief that there are objective criteria of truth that debunk ideology; that appeals to valid interests can be made where individuals are credited with being the best judges on their own behalf, and that ideology has anyway succumbed to a common-sense, reasonable pragmatism. Poststructuralists remain sceptical regarding the possibility of making any such distinctions or claims without getting entangled in the discursive regime that constituted them in the first place.

Returning, finally, to the subject–object dualism that Foucault cites as his second concern about ideology, I suggest that a similar and related series of conflations occurs. The object tends here to be elided with the Real that is off limits, or to a naïve and unmediated experience, while the knowing subject who is mystified but might attain true (class) consciousness is vulnerable to all the anti-humanist and anti-rationalist attacks that poststructuralists rehearse. From this perspective, ideology critique looks dangerously like Cartesian or Kantian idealism, with a disengaged (scientific) subject surveying its objects in order to impose order upon, or elicit order from, reality.

Again, this is a travesty of any dialectical method since for it, subject and object are as much in process as any other phenomena: the way we conceptualise or experience them is historical, not onto-logical or natural. If the rational subject does triumph over its objects in modernity, then this epistemological relation is itself an indication of the material relationship which capitalism actually instantiates; in other words, it is the ideological equivalent of an actual dualism and hierarchy between subject and object. The critical methodology that follows must therefore recognise the historicity both of this relationship and of its own intervention, as well as acknowledging the way both concepts and material conditions are highly dynamic and mutually dependent. I will return to this latter claim shortly, because I think it is crucial in assessing the contemporary relevance and meaning of ideology. But meanwhile it is necessary, having cast some doubt on the reliability of poststructuralist interpretations of dialectics, to see how a more sympathetic account of dialectical methodology and its pursuit of the 'real' might be elicited. For my criticism of the sort of reality/appearance opposition poststructuralists attribute to dialectics is not intended to do away with the distinction altogether. Any retrieval of ideology in its critical sense depends upon it.

DIALECTICS: THE REAL, THE TOTALITY AND THE CRITICAL METHOD

In dialectical references to a reality underlying appearances, a certain reading of Hegel defines the real as the cunning of Reason, as essence, and it is this that Marx allegedly inherits when he alludes to the Truth of History and reveals the reality that ideology occludes. Here is the real as rational versus its deceptive or partial appearances. If however we extricate dialectics as a critical method from this narrative, then the real entails that which is also defined as concrete (as opposed to appearances, which remain abstract). The real is concrete not because it is solidly material but because it is *mediated*. This is indeed what renders it rational, but not in any metaphysical sense.

The reason appearances remain abstract is that while they seem to have common-sense, empirical veracity – as facts, the given – it is actually impossible to say anything about isolated data without recognising their connections with, as well as their differences from, other data. In other words, what looks immediate always turns out to be mediated and the critical method involves tracing this web of connections in order to build an increasingly rich sense of things' significance. This involves their process of genesis, their internal dynamism and trajectory, their inner tensions and vulnerabilities, their potential to transmute into something richer or to disintegrate, their place within an evolving whole. This inquiry is not after all so very different from genealogy and the lessons drawn from Saussurean linguistics, except that the emphasis tends to be on tracing a phenomenology of meaning as opposed to its deconstruction (although even within Marxism, this would be much truer of Merleau-Ponty, for example, than of Adorno).

If one abandons the grand narrative aspect of Hegelianism and accepts history's contingency, then dialectics still permits a hermeneutical project of interpreting the real as this evolving web of material and ideal imbrications – as a field of forces, or what Merleau-Ponty has called the visible and the invisible. Here, for example, is Lukács' account of totality:

> If change is to be understood at all it is necessary to abandon the view that objects are rigidly opposed to each other, it is necessary to elevate their relatedness and the interrelation between these 'relations' and the 'objects' to the same plane of reality. The greater the distance from pure immediacy the larger the net encompassing the 'relations', and the more complete the integration of the 'objects' within the system of relations, the sooner change will cease to be impenetrable and catastrophic, the sooner it will become comprehensible. (Lukács, 1971, p. 154)

Lukács notwithstanding, if such an approach aims towards establishing the totality of connections, their proliferation nevertheless renders this an ongoing critical project, in principle incomplete. I do not think there need be any more sinister definition of totality than this. It is the dialectical, mediated reality, not the impossible Real or the empirical real, full presence, that is at issue. In poststructuralist eyes totality equals the triumph of reason, a universality that suppresses otherness, particularity and nonidentity, in short, totalitarianism. But for dialectical thinkers, it signifies the critical project of interpreting the real from within as it unfolds: both in order to demonstrate its instability and structural significance (versus positivism, empiricism, ideological versions of common sense) and to guide praxis strategically through a reading of the present (like Machiavellian *virtù*). While we can never in principle represent the real completely, faithfully (the positivist goal) since we are situated within it, neither is in an alien domain immune to understanding since it is the outcome of interpersonal acts, where nature itself has been worked over by symbolic and material practices.

To be authentic, any interpretive process must be self-critical, not dogmatic (Merleau-Ponty's hyper-dialectics, Adorno's negative dialectics, Kristeva's semiology); an amalgam of discovery and invention. As Marx put it: 'The concrete is concrete only because it is the concentration of many determinations, hence the unity of the diverse' (Marx, 1973, p. 100). As Balibar adds, what interests Marx is 'the relation of forces in play at any particular moment, determining the direction of its advance' (Balibar, 1995, pp. 100f.). The trick is to sustain a methodology that accommodates both the diversity of particular parts and the shifting identity of the whole; one that does justice both to sociological facts and their significance; to the objective and its interpretation. This was, in fact, the methodology explicitly practised by the early Frankfurt School.

In so far as dialectics speaks of the real here, it is not then making metaphysical claims about the in itself or claiming some privileged knowledge of History's laws; it is not claiming to mirror the Truth of an objective reality through an act of accurate representation. Rather it is interpreting the field of existence from within, making sense of its provisional forms, potentials and vectors, from the perspective of those whom the given configurations of power suppress. While this need not privilege any particular group, it cannot however entail an empowering of just any voice: only those that challenge closures and open up a field of inquiry or coexistence are historically progressive. This is what allows dialectics to avoid dogmatism or relativism. As Merleau-Ponty claims, truth is a blending of perspectives into provisional unities, a bringing of reason into being where it was not predestined; the true is what opens a field for further questioning and exploration, as opposed to the false which closes it down.

This allows falsity to be aligned with ideology in its pejorative sense – it blocks change – without claiming that its antithesis is Truth in some ahistorical, definitive sense where it is devoid of power or perspective. Whether one speaks of ideology or discourse, however, I have claimed that all the approaches involved operate with this basic political distinction between openness and closure, where the ideological involves the processes that block openness, mobility and change in order to protect the interests of currently privileged groups. The aim in all cases is to open a space for new or counter-meanings, where false consciousness would be a closed consciousness, not a failure to recognise true interests or the occlusion of an autonomous subjectivity. This is not a philosophy of subjectivity but of intersubjectivity.

To summarise and recapitulate, then, I have suggested that the major obstacle to retrieving a concept of ideology after poststructuralism lies in the latter's attributing to ideology a true/false opposition which apparently involves it in a series of epistemological errors and metaphysical illusions whose exposure renders ideology untenable. I have however offered something like a genealogy of this poststructuralist argument, suggesting that it draws on a whole series of claims directed against a much bigger target than ideology per se. In the process the dialectical understanding of the real, one which is not necessarily vulnerable to the sort of criticisms poststructuralism raises, gets distorted.

The critical method dialectics supports here is more similar to genealogy than the latter's exponents acknowledge, but it resolves better the basis for a non-dogmatic political and normative judgement which avoids the relativism into which discourse theory is drawn. At the same time, it is less hesitant about interpreting socio-economic reality in order to guide political interventions, while it resists temptations to emphasise singularity and difference at the expense of recognising more pervasive structures and relationships there. External reality in this materialist approach is recognised as exerting a non-discursive pressure which needs to be understood, and the important questions here concern the right sort of sociological methodology (it is no coincidence, for example, that both Adorno and Merleau-Ponty were interested in Weber's approach). These kinds of concern seem to get eclipsed inasmuch as the shift from ideology to discourse and *différance* tends to favour methods of literary criticism.

It is in terms of a dialectical methodology, one which recognises the intimate relationship between changing historical conditions and the necessity of new concepts for analysing them, that I want to make my final remarks.[12] It must be important from this perspective to guard against any reification of the concept of ideology itself. Might it not be the case, as intimated in my introduction, that the term's difficulties are less conceptual than historical? By this I mean that the apparent confusions attributed to the term might arise less from its internal contradictions than from shifts in the conditions to which it is applied.

Now for Marx, ideology related primarily to the realm of ideas: ideas that were not simply a cynical means of propaganda but entire belief systems supporting the status quo. German idealist philosophy and liberal political theory do indeed seem especially appropriate for the maintenance of bourgeois capitalism, which relies on voluntary submission to apparently rational authority or class relations. In other words, it is not just the content of the ideas but their rationalism as such which is particularly fitting. For both capitalism and the liberal state rely upon voluntary compliance rather than coercion, and this is won by appeals to rational self-interest which in turn relies upon (even constitutes) a certain rational subjectivity. So the priority accorded to ideas in sustaining the system, as well as their correspondence with the socio-economic domain, seems historically appropriate.

As structural differentiation proceeds with modernity, so the institutions that disseminate ideas conducive to the system proliferate (schools, mass media, etc.). Additionally, as capitalism develops it is able to reproduce itself more effectively because the sort of performances it requires are integrated into the everyday habits and practices of society, where they become increasingly pervasive. Thus ideology no longer needs to be confined to the ideal and essentially negative realm: it becomes instantiated in material practices that have more constitutive power. This is what Althusser recognised. At the same time, as critical theorists and postmodernists have seen, new technologies allow cultural production to take off in such a way that older spaces for free time or unintegrated ideas are closed off. If critics of ideology or discourse theory complain that it leaves no space for criticism from outside, then this in a sense expresses the new reality.

Accordingly, a dialectical method might suggest that ideology as Marx conceived it *has* become historically anachronistic: not however because he was confused about its nature or function but because the mechanisms for reproducing the system have changed. It is interesting in this context to recall Baudrillard's account of postmodernity, where the true/false and reality/appearance distinction is occluded not because it was philosophically confused, but because conditions in an image-drenched culture have changed. Now it is simulation that threatens the difference between true and false, real and imaginary. Now reality is produced and reproduced by the imaginary. This, Baudrillard tells us, is the ultimate ideology. 'One can live with the idea of a distorted truth', he assures us, but not with the realisation that images conceal nothing: that images are merely simulacra, that is, copies for which no original ever existed. As such, ideology in postmodern cultures permits the production of an illusion of reality in order to uphold an obsolete and illusionary true/false distinction which can no longer be made. Paradoxically, the very idea of ideology comes to play an ideological role at the same time as the distinctions on which it relied disappear (Baudrillard, 1983).

I do not have time now to start unravelling the conundra into which this argument throws us. I have invoked Baudrillard only to support my final suggestion that questions about ideology's meaning and continuing relevance can only be approached in historical context and that the dialectical approach which is associated, through Marx, with ideology is the best way to proceed. No amount of analysis of terminology can substitute for this difficult engagement with the real. What remains is thus a methodology which is broadly a historical materialism infused with elements of genealogy. Whether ideology as a concept remains the most appropriate way of grasping and challenging the maintenance and reproduction of relations of privilege or exclusion here remains a historical and sociological question which awaits the judgement of an ongoing dialectical inquiry.

NOTES

1. The sociological and psychological imperatives that result in a strengthened authoritarianism even where revolt in on the agenda have often been explored. See for example Horkheimer (1982) and Foucault (1983).
2. I pursue this theme in Coole (2000), especially in Chapter 3 and the conclusion. The considerations in this chapter are to some extent a development informed by arguments presented there.
3. Deleuze and Guattari (1994) insist that it is philosophy's utopianism that makes it political. The ethical dimension is explicit throughout most of Derrida's work and also within Foucault's later writing.
4. This is the gist of Habermas's designation of poststructuralists as young conservatives, in his 'Modernity: An Unfinished Project'. The essay has been reprinted many times in English but see the complete translation in Habermas (1996).
5. It is Lyotard who explicitly and famously proffers these two metanarratives, in Lyotard (1984).
6. Although they implicitly oppose dialectical, critical reasoning to the rationalist logic of enlightenment, the equation between reason and totalitarianism had been made by members of the Frankfurt School well before poststructuralism. See in particular Horkheimer and Adorno (1972). See also the section on 'Absolute Freedom and Terror' in Hegel (1967) and Merleau-Ponty (1969).
7. See Deleuze and Guattari (1994). Philosophy creates a plane of immanence which might come to seem like truth although it has nothing to do with the representation of actual states of affairs.
8. Such arguments were perhaps most explicitly developed by the first generation of critical theorists.
9. For more about this see Coole (2000), in particular Chapter 1.
10. For a summary of criticisms of Lukes, see S. Clegg (1989), Chapter 5.
11. R. Gasché (1986, p. 57) writes: 'A totality … amounts to a medium of mediation, a middle of intersecting lines.'

12. This relationship seems to be ruled out by Deleuze and Guattari in *What is Philosophy?* for example, when they distinguish between science's interests in states of affairs and philosophy's conceptual creativity.

REFERENCES

Balibar, E. (1995) *Marx and Philosophy* (London: Verso).
Baudrillard, J. (1983) *Simulations* (New York: Semiotext(e)).
Berlin, I. (1969) 'Two Concepts of Liberty', in *Four Essays on Liberty* (Oxford: Oxford University Press).
Clegg, S. (1989) *Frameworks of Power* (London: Sage).
Coole, D. (2000) *Negativity and Politics: Dionysus and Dialects from Kant to Post-structuralism* (London: Routledge).
Deleuze, G. (1983) *Nietzsche and Philosophy* (London: Athlone Press).
Deleuze, G. (1994) *Difference and Repetition* (London: Athlone Press).
Deleuze, G. and Guattari, F. (1994) *What is Philosophy?* (London: Verso).
Derrida, J. (1981) *Positions* (London: Athlone Press).
Derrida, J. (1982) *Margins of Philosophy* (Hemel Hempstead: Harvester).
Foucault, M. (1972) *Power/Knowledge* (New York: Pantheon Books).
Foucault, M. (1983) 'Preface', in Deleuze, G. and Guattari, F. *Anti-Oedipus* (Minneapolis: University of Minnesota Press).
Gasché, R. (1986) *The Tain of the Mirror* (Cambridge MA: Harvard University Press).
Habermas, J. (1996) 'Modernity: An Unfinished Project', in Passerin D'Entrèves, M. and Benhabib, S. (eds), *Habermas and the Unfinished Project of Modernity* (Cambridge: Polity Press).
Hegel, G.W.F. (1967) *Phenomenology of Mind* (New York: Harper Colophon).
Horkheimer, M. and Adorno, T. (1972) *Dialectic of Enlightenment* (New York: Seabury Press).
Horkheimer, M. (1982) 'The Authoritarian State', in Arato, A *et al.* (eds), *The Essential Frankfurt School Reader* (New York: Continuum).
Lukács, G. (1971) *History and Class Consciousness: Studies in Marxist Dialectics* (Cambridge MA: MIT Press).
Lukes, S. (1974) *Power: A Radical View* (London: Macmillan).
Lyotard, F. (1984) *The Postmodern Condition* (Manchester: Manchester University Press).
Marx, K. (1973) *Grundrisse* (Harmondsworth: Penguin).
Merleau-Ponty, M. (1969) *Humanism and Terror* (Boston: Beacon Press).

7   Ideology, Language and Discursive Psychology

Michael Billig

In a famous passage of *The German Ideology*, Marx and Engels claimed that the study of ideology should begin with the activity of 'real men' (1970, p. 42). They were suggesting that theory on its own was insufficient for understanding how ideology operated. One needed to observe how men (and women) actually live and think. According to Marx and Engels, the social processes of inequality distort the way that the oppressed classes experience the world, so that mentally the world is turned upside down in a way that hides the workings of power. In effect, Marx and Engels were proposing that an understanding of ideology should have an important psychological dimension, for ideology is reflected in the feelings, views and life patterns of 'real' people. Today, it is no longer possible to hold a convincing theory of ideology which simply states that the powerful classes conceal the operations of their power by implanting falsehoods in the minds of the oppressed. Rightly, there has been a reaction against the tendency to reduce the subject of ideology to a 'dupe' who unwittingly accepts the distortions of ideology. A more active view of the ideological subject is required. Even if the theory of ideology outlined in *The German Ideology* is no longer satisfactory in itself, nevertheless the dictum of Marx and Engels should still be taken seriously. Any reconstituted theory of ideology needs to be based on understanding people and, as such, it requires a psychological dimension at its core.

Today, as theorists attempt to reconstitute a theory of ideology that is appropriate for contemporary conditions, two factors tend to be stressed. First, the power of language is often recognised. Following Foucault, it is generally accepted that discourses constrain what people say and think; moreover, discourses are closely related to patterns of social power. Second, theorists today often accept that a theory of ideology should incorporate a psychology of the unconscious, in order to understand how the subjects of ideology have internalised forces of distortion that will curtail, channel or recreate desires, wishes, etc. Many theorists, especially in the field of cultural studies, have found both elements in the work of Lacan, whose motto is that the unconscious is structured like language. Unfortunately, the more that theorists tend to turn to Lacan, the more they find themselves being pulled away from studying 'real' people in the way that Marx and Engels recommended. Lacan's writing is highly abstract and abstruse. Surprisingly for a psychoanalyst, he does not base his theories on accounts of the lives of people. As Stuart Hall (1988, p. 35) has complained, there is today an 'overtheoreticism', which tends to 'pile up one sophisticated theoretical construction on top of another ... without ever once touching ground and without reference to a single concrete case or historical example'.

In contrast, the present chapter will introduce a different form of psychology that is suitable for incorporating into a reconstituted view of ideology. This form of psychology – discursive psychology – acknowledges the importance of language in constituting human thinking (for statements of this position, see for example, Antaki, 1994; Billig, 1991 and 1996; Edwards, 1997; Edwards and Potter, 1993; Harré and Gillett, 1994; Potter, 1996; Potter and Wetherell, 1987). In this respect, discursive psychology fulfils the primary requirement for any theory of ideology: it recognises the extent to which thinking is socially constructed. As such, the discursive approach differs from most orthodox psychological theories that tend to explain thinking in terms of universal properties of the individual (Billig, 1991; Parker, 1992; van Dijk, 1998). In addition, discursive psychology can be extended to show how Freud's theory of the unconscious can be reinterpreted in terms of speech and discourse. Most importantly, discursive psychology is not content to formulate abstract theories, but is based on the detailed study of social actors. Consequently, it seeks to ground any reconstituted theory of ideology in the actions, thoughts and lives of 'real men', as Marx and Engels advocated.

THREE PSYCHOLOGICAL LEVELS

Three levels of psychological functioning can be distinguished: the conscious, the routine and the unconscious. A psychology which is satisfactory for a theory of ideology must be able to deal with these three levels and, moreover, show their interrelations even within a single activity. It will be suggested that all three levels can be manifested simultaneously within the business of talk.

(a) The conscious level. Much conscious thinking is directly shaped within language, for we use language to think. Every day we make new utterances; our use of language is creative. It will be suggested that the argumentative aspects of language are fundamental for this creativity.

(b) The routine level. Language use is not, and cannot just be, a matter of individual creativity. We inherit languages and have to use accepted social codes in order to engage in the social activity of talk. As Gramsci wrote in the *Prison Notebooks* (1971), languages contain their own philosophies, often expressed as a shared common sense, which is taken for granted. In this sense, language can mould its speaker's thoughts in particular directions, with the result that some matters are routinely spoken about and other topics are left unspoken – indeed, they cannot be spoken about. This latter aspect of language has been well studied by Foucault and his followers. They show how a society's discursive concepts are integrated into that society's patterns of life. Some matters are routinely accepted as common sense, while other topics, for which the requisite concepts have not been formulated, are literally unspeakable. Thus, in the Middle Ages, speakers lacked the discursive resources to talk about psychiatric matters. Today, so prevalent are these discourses, that contemporary speakers at times find it hard to avoid speaking psychiatrically.

(c) The unconscious level. There is an aspect of the 'unsaid' which Foucauldians tend not to examine. They examine that which cannot be spoken because the speakers lack the necessary discursive resources. However, there is another form of 'unsaid'. These are matters that could be spoken about – the discursive resources are in place. Nevertheless, there are silences, because social taboos demand that some topics be repressed from outward conversation and inner thought. In order to understand this sort of unsaid there is a need to turn to Freud and to reinterpret his notion of repression dialogically.

THE NATURE OF THINKING

To begin with, it is necessary to outline briefly the discursive approach to the topic of 'conscious thinking' (for more details, see Antaki, 1994; Billig, 1991, 1996 and 1999a; Edwards, 1997; Edwards and Potter, 1993). Orthodox psychologists, particularly contemporary cognitive psychologists, typically take a Cartesian approach to the study of thinking. They assume that thinking is a silent, solitary (even lonely) activity, which takes place mysteriously within the brain of the isolated individual. Thus, the psychologist cannot directly observe the processes of thinking, but must infer their existence from outward behaviour. This Cartesian view of thinking, as an internal and individual activity, is exemplified by Rodin's famous sculpture *The Thinker*. Rodin depicts a man (of course, a man – not a woman), sitting alone, with forehead resting on his hand. He is not talking, nor paying attention to anyone. All his attention is directed inwards, as if he is removed from active social life. The image suggests that thinking is not a social, discursive activity, but is something solitary and silent.

There are psychological problems with this image of thinking. Any psychology, based on this image, will lack an observable object of study. Its topics, whether they be 'attitudes', 'memory stores' or 'heuristic processes', will be ghostly entities, which, however powerful the methodological microscope, can never be directly observed. Cognitive psychology, like much of psychology, is a strange scientific discipline: its objects of study, which are the presumed 'cognitive processes' underlying thought, are inherently unobservable, for these hypothetical processes are not assumed to be neurological structures (Harré and Gillett, 1994).

There is another factor, which should concern those involved in education. The traditional view of thinking, as a wordless, soundless process, seems to imply that the thinking of other people is always out of reach. We may know our own thinking, but we can never know the thinking of other people. If thinking is this solitary, private activity, then we can ask how is it possible to teach thinking? According to the Cartesian view, it is hard to see how children can be taught to think, for thinking cannot be demonstrated. It must be something that mysteriously develops within the individual psyche, untouched by conversation or social contact.

As Wittgenstein repeatedly argued in his later philosophical writings, another position is possible (for discussions of the relations between Wittgenstein's ideas and discursive psychology, see, in particular, Shotter, 1993a and 1993b). Thinking can be seen as a social, and above all, discursive, activity. Of course, this idea well pre-dates Wittgenstein. It was well expressed by the Eleatic Stranger, in Plato's dialogue *The Sophist*: 'Thought and speech are the same; only the former, which is the silent inner conversation of the soul with itself, has been given the special name of thought' (263 e).

This could be applied to Rodin's solitary thinker. Far from being removed from dialogue, he might be imagined to be conducting an internal dialogue, debating with himself in an example of what the Russian psychologist Lev Vygotsky termed 'inner speech' (Vygotsky, 1987; see also Wertsch, 1991; Sampson, 1993). Such an internal conversation, given the thinker's outward signs of preoccupation, will probably have an argumentative character. He is unlikely to have divided his mind into two speakers, only to find them in happy agreement – as if his desire says, 'I want to get off this rock and go for an ice cream' and his voice of conscience replies 'what a lovely idea'. Were this the case, he would not still be sitting on the rock, head on hand.

Instead, we can imagine a fierce debate inside his head, turning over the pros and cons of a course of action. Perhaps the voices of desire and conscience are vigorously debating a course of action or the ethics of another's personality. Maybe, seated on his seaside rock, he is debating whether, despite doctor's advice, to go for that ice cream. Whatever the content of the internal debate, one might say that Rodin's thinker-as-debater has not been abstracted totally from social life. Instead, his internal processes would be derived from publicly observable debate, as he uses, silently and internally, a public language. He must have observed and participated in debates, and, thus, have acquired the skills of debate, or argument. Only if he has done so can he sit there alone, arguing with himself.

This would imply that the skills of debate, or argument, are vital for much of our thinking. To think about ethics, politics or human character – in short, the questions which preoccupy social life – we need the skills of language. Central to language are the skills of argument, for language is not merely a device for naming objects or representing external reality. Language provides the means of justification and criticism, and most notably the faculty for negation. Indeed, a means of communication without negation, and without the resources for justification and criticism, would scarcely qualify to be a language (Billig, 1996).

Of all species which can communicate to fellow members, only humans have the faculty for negation and, thereby, for argumentation. Other species can process visual information, recognise sounds and remember to orientate to particular shapes. Chimpanzees can even be taught to use sign language. But however much effort is spent developing the linguistic skills of chimpanzees with sign language, there is a ceiling. No psychologist has been able to teach a chimpanzee to justify and criticise argumentatively. Only humans, equipped with the syntax of negation, can do these things. As such, dialogic thinking, or the conduct of internal debate, is something that is pre-eminently human.

THE STUDY OF THINKING

The linking of human thought to the use of language has a number of implications for the sort of psychology that is being proposed by discursive psychologists. In the first place, discursive psychology recommends that the traditional topics of psychology should be studied discursively. If psychological states are constituted within and by discursive practices, then psychologists, instead of looking within the head of the isolated individual, should be directing their attention to the activities of discourse. This does not mean examining the linguistic structure of language conceived as a total structure, but looking at the actual, messy business of speech and conversation. For this reason, many discursive psychologists have adopted the methods of micro-sociology, in particular conversation analysis.

This can be illustrated with respect to the topic of memory. Traditionally psychologists have searched inside the mind for hypothetical memory stores. Discursive psychologists, on the contrary, claim that this is to look in the wrong place. Human memory is not merely, or even principally, about retaining stimuli. It is about performing social actions, such as remembering a birthday, remembering one's manners or remembering the sacrifices of past generations. There is a whole range of activities which we call 'remembering', or 'forgetting'. Discursive psychologists claim that we should investigate what activities are called 'remembering' and how these activities are accomplished in social life. Above all, discursive psychology examines the claims people make to remember or forget things, and to see what they are doing in making such claims. One of the findings of discursive psychology is that people making memory claims are typically not reporting on inner states, but doing other things (Edwards, 1997; Potter and Edwards, 1990; Middleton and Edwards, 1990). For example, if someone, on returning from a trip, says to their partner 'I did remember you all the time I was away', they are unlikely to be making a simple report of an internal state. Instead, the memory claim itself will be an action which is accomplishing important interactional business.

The same move of looking at the outward behaviour, rather than the hypothesised internal structure, can be seen in relation to a topic which has traditionally been central to social psychology – the study of attitudes. The discursive/rhetorical approach directs the psychologist's attention to the dynamics of debate. One can see 'the holding of attitudes' in terms of taking stances in matters of public controversy. Moreover, in participating in debate, people typically are engaging in thinking, rather than outwardly expressing a preformed, unchanging inner cognitive structure. In debates, and more generally in conversations, people say novel things, making utterances which in their detail have never been made before. Even when talk returns to familiar themes, which the participants may have discussed previously, it seldom, if ever, returns in exactly the same ways (Billig, 1991). Every day, people formulate sentences which they have never said before, and, indeed, which no one else has ever precisely uttered before. In this respect, dialogic creativity is a mundane, even banal, factor of the human condition.

It is hard to account for this mundane creativity, if analysts are too cognitive or, indeed, too Foucauldian. Discourses, conceived as total ideological structures, cannot constrain thinking absolutely, if speakers are routinely formulating new utterances for new situations. There must be some slippage between the hypothetical structure of *la langue* and the actual business of talk. By the same token, it is too simple to assume that our utterances are expressions of internal cognitive processes, which must precede the utterances. Dialogue takes place too quickly to assume that the outer pattern is merely a reflection of something more important taking place internally. Given that people are readily formulating new utterances as they debate issues, then in debate the processes of thinking are directly hearable. By studying the micro-processes of talk, psychologists can directly observe, or hear, the social activity of thinking itself. In this way, the psychologist can see how human thinking is rhetorically accomplished and contested. What was formally assumed to be hidden, indeed mysterious, can be directly studied in its complexity.

There is a further implication in taking this discursive position. It is possible to see how thinking is learnt. If thinking is modelled on conversation, then the child's entry into dialogue is an entry into thinking. Language is not learnt in order that the child can possess a system of naming, or even to represent the outside world. Language is learnt in order that children can participate in the conversations, and thus the social activity, that surround their lives. From the earliest age, adults are speaking to them, telling them things, commenting on their infantile reactions. As children learn to respond, so they learn how to enter this rhetorical world of justification and criticism. Moreover, they do not merely acquire the formal syntax of argument, but they learn what counts as persuasive justification and criticism, as adults and older children offer 'convincing' arguments why certain things should, or should not be, performed. From a comparatively early age, children acquire the skills to challenge arguments and contest the rhetoric they hear (Dunn, 1988).

In all this learning, the child is not merely acquiring the rudiments of language, but of human thinking; the lessons can be transferred or internalised from outer dialogue into inner dialogue, so that children learn to conduct their own internal dialogues or thoughts, like Rodin's thinker. The movement, thus, is from the outer, social world of conversation into the inner world of thought, not vice versa.

RHETORIC AND COMMONPLACES

Argumentation can be conceived as a dialectic of justification and criticism. As a speaker justifies their own position, they criticise the other's position and vice versa (Billig, 1996). However, as Perelman and Olbrechts-Tyteca argued in the pathfinding *The New Rhetoric* (1971), the discourse of argumentation is not simple. Speakers typically do not use a rhetoric that simply addresses the anti-*logoi* of the opponent. In seeking to persuade and to substantiate their criticisms and justifications, they appeal to a 'universal audience'. They speak as if their reasoning is reasonable in an absolute sense, as if any reasonable person, not just the particular addressee, would be persuaded. As such, they use rhetoric which appears to be addressed to the mythical universal audience – or, to use the phrase of Bakhtin, speakers address themselves to a 'super-addressee' (Bakhtin, 1986). This general rhetorical point is substantiated by detailed study of actual conversation, in which speakers argue for their attitudinal positions (Schiffrin, 1984; Billig, 1991). Such speakers not only use a discourse of 'multisubjectivity', which suggests that opinions are subjective and, thus, equally valid, but simultaneously they argue as if there is 'intersubjectivity', such that their own position is 'rationally' superior to those of others.

In arguing, speakers typically employ rhetorical devices which classical rhetoricians identified as 'commonplaces'. These are values, maxims and clichés that speakers assume that they share in common with their fellow speakers. In discourse, these maxims are used to justify particular stances. Because their sense is commonly shared, the maxims themselves do not need to be justified. Speakers can use them as if they are self-evidently 'common sense' or good sense. The communal sense of the particular speakers – their common, shared, sense – appears as *le bon sens*, even as they dispute this commonality. In this way, the two meanings of 'common sense' become conflated in dialogic practice. This rhetorical move makes what is contingent appear as 'natural'. According to theorists such as Eagleton (1991), the transforming of the contingent into the natural is one of the characteristic functions of ideology.

In contemporary political discourse, words such as 'freedom', 'democracy', 'community' act as commonplaces. Not only are they commonly used, but their desirability is assumed to be commonly shared. Speakers will not need to justify 'freedom', but will assume its commonsensical positive value. They will, therefore, try to promote their particular position as enhancing 'freedom', or 'democracy', and that of their opponents as restricting these self-evident desiderata. As such, rhetorical commonplaces – or the unjustified maxims of justification – can convey the ideological assumptions of a speaking community.

The existence of rhetorical commonplaces illustrates something more general about the nature of common sense and ideology. In argumentation, commonplaces are typically brought into opposition, one against another. The ancient textbooks of rhetoric, such as *Rhetorica Ad Herennium*, provided novice orators with lists of suitable commonplaces to be used in particular sorts of debates. For instance, prosecutors were provided with handy maxims about 'justice', whereas defenders were equipped with useful phrases about the need for 'mercy'; or political debaters were given the rhetorical wherewithal to argue for boldness or for prudence.

These rhetorical guidebooks illustrate that common sense is not a unitary structure, whose values are arranged in a consensually agreed hierarchy of importance. Instead, in legal, political and daily life, common sense's common values are continually coming into opposition with each other. The defending counsel might appeal to mercy and the prosecution to justice. Both will be presuming that the jury, or judge, value both mercy and justice. Similarly, political audiences will acknowledge both prudence and boldness as desirable. In fact, most proverbs come in opposite pairs. In English, 'look before you leap' is matched by 'a stitch in time'; 'many hands make light work' can be counterposed by 'too many cooks spoil the broth'.

Such contrary values of common sense are held by the same persons. Juries do not split into those who only love 'mercy' and hate 'justice' and vice versa. In short, common sense provides the rhetorical resources for dilemmas. Speakers argue whether this particular case should be treated as one suitable for mercy or justice, not whether mercy or justice are desirable in the abstract. If the rhetorical commonplaces are seen as ideological constructions, then one might talk of ideological dilemmas (Billig *et al.*, 1988). Ideologies do not dictate exactly what should be thought, thereby excluding the necessity for thoughtful debate. Their very contrary themes ensure the necessity for argumentation, continual debate and the daily formulation of novel utterances. In this respect, ideologies are not coherent systems of belief, but they constantly create dilemmas. Thus, they enable, as well as demand, thinking. Simultaneously the thinking is restricted. Speakers will use the rhetorical resources to hand – they will be constrained by what passes for common sense in their particular community. But in using these resources, they will have to formulate new utterances, adapting the old maxims to new situations, and, thereby, adding to, and perhaps altering, the shared rhetoric.

RHETORICAL ROUTINES

In debating, speakers are consciously aware that they are talking, arguing, responding, etc. In this sense, the thinking that is revealed in argumentative debate is conscious thought. Similarly, the internal debates of inner speech are presumed to be conscious. In consequence, the psychology of argumentation is, at least in the first instance, a psychology of conscious thought. On the other hand, the results of conversation analysis reveal that even the most simple snatches of conversation are extraordinarily rich in their detail: routine greetings or bidding farewell are complexly managed and executed pieces of turn-taking (Nofsinger, 1991; Psathas, 1995). So rich are these exchanges that it makes sense to say that speakers are not consciously aware of all they are doing in conversation. We may not be aware of the exact nature of our hand gestures, pitch or facial expression – nevertheless all these will convey information to the addressee. If speakers are asked to repeat themselves, it is rare, if not impossible, for them to repeat exactly the original utterance: not only may the small words be changed, but so may speed of delivery, intonation, stress, etc.

In short, much of what is accomplished in conversation is done routinely. The codes of turn-taking, for example, are executed as 'second nature'. Discursively, they are part of what Bourdieu (1990) has called the 'habitus' (see Billig, 1999a, for details of this argument). One might presume that ideology is present in the routine, habitual aspects of dialogue. For instance, forms of address and patterns of turn-taking may routinely ascribe speakers with differing statuses and discursive positions (Billig, 1999b). This might be accomplished unthinkingly through routine deictic utterances, which ascribe identities by means of words such as 'we', 'you' and 'them'. In this regard, ideology might be reproduced through the routine, unnoticed small words of conversation.

The small, banal words of nationalism might provide an example. Nationalism is more than a matter of waving flags, imagining historic myths and consciously declaring loyalty. It has its banal aspects (see Billig, 1995, for more details). For established nations such as the United States, Britain and France to be reproduced as nation states and for their inhabitants to remember their national identity, there must be daily reminders of nationhood, often operating below the level of outward conscious awareness. For example, the majority of national flags are not consciously waved or saluted. In the United States, for example, they are hanging outside public buildings or are stitched onto the uniforms of public servants. They are not to be consciously noticed, but, out of the corner of the eye, they constantly flag nationhood, maintaining the physical environment as a national space.

Little words function in the same way. Democratic politicians routinely address the imagined national audience. As they consciously talk on a particular issue – such as taxation, law or the failings of rivals – they will use the little word 'we', often conflating 'we', the party, 'we', the nation, and 'we', all right-thinking people (Billig, 1995; Wilson, 1990). Even more banally, nationhood is indicated in 'neutral' discourses such as weather forecasting. 'The' weather is typically assumed to be the national weather, illustrated in newspapers and on television by maps of the nation. 'We', who are presumed to suffer snow or enjoy sunshine, will be assumed to be a national 'we' (see Billig, 1995 for details).

Thus, nationhood is often flagged in daily discourse, as the attention is directed elsewhere. Readers of weather forecasts may not be consciously aware of nationhood as they consciously absorb the meteorological messages. Yet, at a level below conscious awareness, nationhood is being reproduced. If this psychological level is called 'unconscious', then this is not a Freudian unconscious, for nothing is being repressed. Attention could be directed to the small words and their deictic meaning spelled out. There are no psychological forces preventing this.

UNCONSCIOUS REPRESSION

Freudian repression refers to thoughts that have been repressed from conscious awareness and which are maintained outside of conscious awareness by some sort of resistance. Although Freud considered the notion of repression to be the key concept of psychoanalytic thought, he actually had little to say about how we go about the business of repressing thoughts and, in particular, how we acquire the skills of repression. In order to rectify this gap in Freud, it has been proposed that the notions of discursive psychology be extended in order to see how the unconscious can be created dialogically (see Billig, 1997a and 1999a, for more details). Of course, unconscious repression is a major issue for any theory of ideology, for it draws attention to issues that are collectively avoided in dialogue. If it makes sense to talk of a dialogic unconscious, then it is necessary to show how language is inherently both expressive and repressive – and how we must learn to repress routinely in order to talk routinely.

The possibility of a dialogic, or rhetorically accomplished, unconscious implies that discourse analysts must observe both what is talked about in conversation and what is not talked about. It can be assumed that, on occasion, speakers are involved in a joint activity of avoidance, so that particular ways of talking are repressed dialogically. An example of such avoidance can be given, taken from a study investigating how English families talked about the British royal family (for details of the study, see Billig, 1992). The study involved listening to families talk about royal issues in their own homes. The speakers rarely raised the issue of race, particularly in respect to the question whether the heir to the throne might marry a non-white person. The very issue raised difficult issues for white supporters of the royal family, who saw the monarchy as symbol of nation and identified with the monarch as the representation of their own national identity. Such supporters could not say that the monarch must always be white, for that would risk the accusation of racism. Nor, for the same reasons, could they say that they could not identify with non-white as the epitome of 'Britishness'. Moreover, they could not say that the Queen would disapprove of a non-white daughter-in-law (or son-in-law), for that would suggest that the Queen was racist, and also that the speakers themselves, in identifying with a racist figurehead, were themselves racist.

Instead, the speakers tended to adopt ambiguous ways of talking when the issue was raised. They would talk about an amorphous 'them', saying 'they would not allow it', leaving unsaid who 'they' were. Or they might say that 'the public' would not stand for it, as if they themselves were not part of that public. It was as if they were projecting their own unacceptable wishes onto unspecified others. Above all, awkward questions were not asked by the other members of the family. It is as if all speakers conspired dialogically to protect each other and to protect the projections. In this sense, the avoidance was dialogically constructed and protected.

CONVERSATION AND PRACTICAL MORALITY

A sense of morality typically accompanies dialogic interaction. Harold Garfinkel (1967), founder of ethnomethodology, claimed that, in studying the micro-processes of social life, he was investigating 'practical morality'. This can be seen in 'turn-taking', to which conversation analysts have given much attention. In order for conversation to take place, there have to be complex codes about how speakers alternate their 'turns', by yielding turns, taking up implied invitations to speak, interrupting without disruption and so on. If these unwritten, but daily practised, rules are transgressed, the risk is not merely the breakdown of the immediate interaction, but also a moral evaluation: speakers will accuse the transgressor of transgressing the morality of interaction.

This can be illustrated hypothetically by the codes for asking questions. There is a lot of evidence that questions which are requests will normally be phrased with 'indirection' in American and European conversations, where direct questions will appear rude or aggressive (Brown and Levinson, 1987). This can be seen in academic seminars. At question time, critical questioners are expected to preface their remarks with phrases such as, 'I was fascinated to hear what you said about X, I wonder if you have fully taken into account ...' or 'I was interested in your remarks about Y but was a bit concerned that you didn't mention the work of ...'. If critical questions are raised too directly or intellectual dissatisfaction expressed without any credit being expressed, then others are likely to suggest that the moral codes of politeness have been breached and that rudeness has been performed.

Practically every utterance, if delivered inappropriately, carries the possibility of moral censure. If we pitch our voice too high or too loudly, if we intervene too quickly or too slowly, then we run the risk of being seen to infringe the codes of politeness. As such, every day we habitually practice this conversational morality. As we make habitual utterances which have never been said before, we run the risk of transgressing the morality which permits such utterance.

This view of morality, as being something which is routinely accomplished in dialogue, could be allied to the Freudian view. For Freud, the presence of moral restrictions is a sign of the presence of temptation and desire. If there were no temptation, suggested Freud, then there would be no reason for moral codes. Moreover, according to Freud, temptations not only have to be resisted but often they must be repressed: we cannot admit to ourselves that we have the desires which we regularly resist, and so the temptations, which morality forbids, must be pushed from consciousness.

A Freudian, viewing the complex codes of conversation and turn-taking, should ask what conversational temptations all these codes are being directed against. If complex codes are inbuilt into every utterance, then the Freudian would see temptations as being ever-present. The stronger the codes, the more they suggest the pervasiveness of resisted temptation. Thus, the daily accomplishment of conversation is being stalked by shameful hidden desire and temptation. One might say that ordinary talk, conventionally considered as 'polite', is somehow keeping at bay, or even repressing, the temptation of rudeness.

There are reasons for supposing that the possibility of speaking politely depends on being able to speak rudely (see Billig, 1997a and 1999a for more details). Politeness is not a biological imperative, but children have to learn its codes and intonations. The paradox is that as children learn the codes of politeness so they learn how to be rude. Parents, or other adults, are frequently correcting children for inappropriate talking. They often utter words to the effect of 'don't say that, it's rude'. In speaking thus the adult is doing two things: they are indicating what is polite (how to speak) and also what is rude (what should not be spoken). Moreover, they are doing it in a conventionally rude way. Parents tend to talk to children in direct ways which are unacceptable in adult conversation (for details see Billig 1999a). 'Don't say that, it's rude' is not typically the sort of utterance to be made in adult polite conversation. Thus, an adult, in so speaking to a child, is not just indicating what rude talk is, but the adult is exemplifying rudeness. Therefore, as the child learns politeness, it also learns to acquire the dangerous weapons of rudeness. Indeed, it is not possible to have one without the other.

Studies of mother–child interaction show that the teaching of language, morality and polite behaviour is not smooth (Dunn, 1988). Between the ages of two and three especially, young children deliberately challenge and resist the authority of the mother. Above all, the breaking of rules is a matter of enjoyment, especially those rules forbidding talk about bodily functions or the making of rude remarks. This suggests something of which Freud was well aware – there is pleasure in rudeness. As the child becomes older and is expected to enter the world of mature conversation, such pleasure must be curtailed. Adult speakers cannot talk as a two-year-old, but must become responsible and polite. Thus, politeness demands the repression of rudeness and of childish jokes. In Freudian terms, what is repressed is desired; it is an object of temptation. In this respect, the learning of dialogue creates pleasures and desires, which the child must learn to repress or 'grow out of'.

It might be objected that 'repressing' and 'growing out' of pleasures are two very different things. If we grow out of the pleasures, then we stop desiring those pleasures: they no longer attract us. But if we repress those childish pleasures, we secretly still desire them, but we deny these desires even to ourselves. The question to ask is what evidence is there that the pleasures of rudeness are repressed, rather than grown out of.

From a Freudian perspective, the most direct evidence comes from jokes. As Freud realised in *Jokes and Their Relation to the Unconscious* many jokes derive their humour from the fact that they express repressed desires, especially those relating to sex and aggression. Many of the great comic heroes, from Diogenes of Sinope to Groucho Marx and John Cleese, are unspeakably rude. Instead of being outraged by their displays of breaking the restricting codes of politeness, onlookers greet their antics with loud signs of pleasure. It is as if we would like to do what the comic does. John Cleese, as Basil Fawlty, not only insults the guests in his hotel, but he mocks the rules of politeness by insulting through overpoliteness. Because the joke is merely a joke, the release is safe – the rules are in fact strengthened by their breach being defined as just a joke.

There are several implications which can be drawn from this linkage of conversation and the idea of repression:

(a) Adult conversation is restricting: it makes demands on talkers. Codes of turn-taking, which are necessary for the activity of dialogue, must be routinely followed and enacted in conversation.

(b) These dialogic codes of politeness create the possible pleasures of rudeness, which if continually put into practice would make language as a social activity impossible.

(c) Desires to break the routine codes of conversation must be repressed or driven from the mind. If speakers are conscious of the desire to be rude (for example to shout 'Mr Piggyface' to one's fellow conversationalist) then they will be unable carry on routine, habitual conversations.

(d) In consequence, the child who learns to be a moral, ordinary speaker, must learn to repress.

(e) This involves not merely repressing the desire to be rude, but also learning to avoid disturbing subjects, by changing topics, etc., for the mature speaker must learn the routine rhetoric of dialogic avoidance.

(f) In consequence, the repression of desire is basic to language. As such language is not merely expressive, but it is repressive.

(g) If, in learning to participate in dialogue, the child must learn to repress, then the child acquires skills of repression that later in life can be applied inwardly to drive out uncomfortable thoughts. Thus the skills of repression can parallel the skills of thinking: what the child first learns in outward debate can later be used in the dialogues of inner thinking.

FREUD'S CASES

Freud's classic case histories can be reinterpreted in the light of discursive psychology's insistence on paying attention to the 'small' words of dialogue (for details of these reinterpretations, see Billig, 1997c, 1998, 1999a, 1999c). Not only do these cases bear rereading for the light they continue to throw upon enduring issues in psychoanalytic theory (Spence, 1994), they also illustrate a further point in relation to the idea that the unconscious is dialogically produced. If language is repressive, then even Freud's own texts may have their hidden or repressive aspects. More particularly, in drawing attention to repression, and in revealing its hidden aspects, Freud may have also been engaging in repressive activity himself. And this repression may also be in line with wider ideological factors.

One aspect of the case histories that has particular interest for a discursive psychologist is Freud's accounts of his own dialogues with his patients. Freud was especially interested in the 'big' symbolism contained in his patient's words. A discursive psychologist, by contrast, might look towards the details of dialogue which Freud seems to ignore. This is notable in the case of Little Hans, the young child whose development provided Freud with direct evidence for the Oedipus complex (Freud, 1990a). Freud's account concentrates on Hans's desires, most notably his sexual desires for his mother and aggressive impulses towards his father. According to Freud, Hans represses both sets of desires. However, if Freud's account is read carefully, especially in relation to the notes which Hans's father takes of conversations with his young son, it is possible to see more than the young child's desires. It is possible to hear his parents talking to him, often changing the subject, when Hans asks awkward questions. The parents are instructing him into the conventions of morality, telling him to be ashamed of certain wishes, to behave and to speak appropriately; they can even be heard to project their own desires onto Hans, as jealous parents, denying their own jealousy and teaching the young boy to believe that he is being unfairly jealous (Billig, 1998). In this way, Hans learns that some things are to be talked about and others are shameful. He learns discursive devices for changing the topics of conversation, and these discursive devices can be used to change the topics of his own internal thoughts (for details, see Billig, 1999a).

SEXUALITY, POLITENESS AND DORA

Freud's case histories suggest that it is the sexual which is, above all, forbidden and is not to be discussed openly. But there is a paradox: Freud in his texts discusses sex openly; Hans's parents are Freudians – they are constantly bringing up sexual themes; and in psychoanalytic interviews, sex is talked about. Freud saw this as a liberation from repression, with the texts of psychoanalysis providing a non-repressive form of discourse in which nothing is hidden. Yet, if language is repressive, then these texts, which are so open about sexuality, might be drawing attention away from other matters, of which it was even more difficult to speak. In other words, Freud's own texts might be creating their own silences.

This can be illustrated by a slightly earlier case than that of Little Hans – the celebrated case of Dora, which Freud published as 'Fragment of analysis of case of hysteria' in 1905 (for full details of the analysis, see Billig, 1997c and 1999a). Dora, a young woman of 18, was showing symptoms of hysteria. Her family situation was complex, as her family's life was intertwined with that of another family, the Ks. Dora's father, a domineering man, who insisted that his daughter consult Dr Freud, was having an affair with Frau K. Dora regularly looked after Frau K's children. Her father was regularly conspiring that the two families spend time together and share holidays. Herr K had been pursuing Dora since she was 14. On occasion, he had even grabbed her, tried to kiss her, and entered her bedroom on holiday. At last Dora told her father about Herr K's advances. Her father refused to believe her. Dora had been greatly distressed and had threatened suicide. Her father had wanted Dr Freud to cure her of this nonsense.

Freud sought to fulfil his remit by locating the cause of Dora's 'pathology' in her unconscious wishes, rather than in her family circumstance. He claimed that she really loved Herr K (which she denies and which Freud takes as sign of resistance). Also, he later suggested that she had lesbian desires for Frau K, which likewise had been repressed.

Feminist critics have recently criticised Freud for taking an apolitical stance towards Dora, and ignoring the politics of the family (see Billig, 1997c and 1999a for details). However, they, in common with Freud, can be said also to be apolitical, in that their analyses avoid the outward politics of the time. Freud's original case report did not mention that both the doctor and the patient were Jewish (many of today's critics overlook the political significance of this). This might not seem a relevant detail for a psychoanalytic report today but at the time Vienna was a deeply anti-Semitic society. Its elected mayor, Karl Lueger, was an anti-Semitic demagogue, whose party had promised to sack all Jewish doctors.

At the time when Freud treated Dora, he was at the most isolated point of his life. He believed he had failed to gain promotion at the University of Vienna because of anti-Semitism. There were regular boycotts of lectures by Jewish academics. Freud himself had withdrawn from lecturing, even to fellow doctors. His only regular audience was the B'nai B'rith, the Jewish defence organisation.

Dora's family, like that of Freud, were assimilating Jews, who looked forward to joining mainstream society (see Decker, 1991, for details). As with many bourgeois Jews in the Vienna of that time, these hopes included an identification with German culture. It was a painful identification, for the culture was deeply anti-Semitic.

Sometimes, bourgeois Jews ignored the anti-Semitism of the culture with which they were identifying. Sometimes they took on such assumptions, directing them against *Ostjuden*, or eastern, non-German-speaking Jews, as if they themselves were not really Jewish, but the eastern Jews were the real Jews, and the ones to criticise. One might say that an avoidance was built into the routines of life and conversation.

This avoidance, which was part of the ideological climate of those times, even reached into the dialogic routines of Freud's consulting room. It is not merely that Freud and Dora do not seem to have talked about the political situation of the time (Decker, 1991). Perhaps that is unsurprising. After all, it is in the nature of psychoanalytic conversations that the topics are personal rather than political. Dora seems to have understood the conversational game. She appears to have talked readily without undue inhibition. However, there is one point at which the conversation appears to have come unstuck, as Freud asks a question and Dora avoids replying.

The moment comes when Freud is interpreting the dream, which in the published report is presented as 'the second dream'. Dora says that she dreamt of going to a strange town. She meets a strange man and asks him the way to the railway station. She is trying to return home, because she has heard that her father has died and that all the family are at the cemetery. Freud interprets the dream in terms of shameful desires. He claims that the underlying meaning is based on Dora's wish to kill her father, in order to be free to engage in sexual activity. In constructing this interpretation, Freud brilliantly makes connections between the German words for cemetery, station and female sexual organs.

Given that Freud claimed that dreams were 'over-determined', or have multiple meanings, it is rather surprising that he misses obvious religious interpretations. He does not offer an interpretation which suggests that Dora wishes to be freed from her father's traditions, in order to marry a stranger, or non-Jew. Jewish themes are indicated by the phrase 'the cemetery', to which the rest of the family have gone. 'The' cemetery, in this context, would be assumed to be a Jewish cemetery (in fact, a year after Freud's report was published, Dora, by now married, converted to Protestantism, along with her husband and infant child).

The most remarkable incident of all occurs when Freud asks about the strange town in which Dora dreams she is wandering. He links the town to Dresden, which she had previously visited. She describes that visit, mentioning that she visited the art gallery. Freud inquires about the visit. Dora replies that she stood in front of Raphael's pictures of the Madonna for two hours. Freud then asks the seemingly obvious and innocuous question: what had she liked about the picture?

It is at this point that the conversation breaks down. Freud reports that she could give no clear answer to his question. Finally, she answers, 'The Madonna'. Most surprisingly Freud does not ask why she was stuck for an answer. Nor in his report does he present it as a problem. Quite the contrary, he seems to dismiss the incident, mentioning in a footnote that Dora seems to be showing an identification with the Madonna, and that this represents a culturally approved desire for motherhood and thus, a guilt-free desire for sexual intercourse. Freud does not apparently see the contradiction in this analysis: if the identification is culturally acceptable, then why should there be such hesitation?

Of course, the identification in this case was not culturally acceptable. Freud does not discuss the symbolic meaning of a Jewish girl staring at the Madonna, as if identifying with the mother of Jesus. If her staring indicates a wish to be a mother, it is a Christian mother (as, in fact, she became). A whole complex of issues, touching on guilt, betrayal and self-hatred, is involved. But Freud in his report avoids all this, just as he and Dora in their conversation had apparently done. It was easier to talk (and write) of sexual matters than it was to speak of other things.

This does not reflect the personal psychology of Freud and Dora. It is a message of their times and conditions of life. The repressed themes were part of habits of avoidance, which were maintained by routine conversations leading in other directions. If the embarrassing topic should intrude (as it does following Freud's question about the Madonna), then after a momentary embarrassment conversation is directed along other paths, and all is forgotten. But, as with Freudian repression, what is forgotten is not obliterated, never to return, but leaves its trace.

Perhaps it is no coincidence that the greatest psychological theory of self-deception was developed at a time and place when an element of collective self-deception was built into conditions of life. In such conditions, avoidance can seem natural and rational. By contrast, too unbending a gaze, or too voiced a sentiment, might be taken as a sign of irrationality. This is illustrated by a story from Freud's own family circle.

The youngest of Freud's five sisters, Adolphine, was considered sweet, oversensitive and slightly dotty by the rest of the family. Sigmund, in one of his letters to his wife, had said she had 'such a great capacity for deep feeling and alas an all-too-fine sensitiveness'. Sigmund's son Martin, years later, was to write how she used to imagine insults as she walked along the streets. Other members of the family put this down to her silliness, verging on paranoia. She would say 'Did you hear what that man said? He called me a dirty stinking Jewess and said it was time we were all killed' (see M. Freud, 1957, p. 16). It was rather a joke with the other Freuds.

Today, it is not possible to dismiss Adolphine. In the most awful way, she was proved correct. Years later, when the Nazis invaded Vienna, Freud was able to escape in time. So too was Dora, whom Freud had not seen for years. But Adolphine and three other sisters had no escape, being taken to the camps from which they were never to return. Even Sigmund Freud, justifiably praised for hearing things which few previously had dared to hear, had not been able to bring himself to hear what his youngest sister not only heard, but had understood.

REFERENCES

Antaki, C. (1994) *Explaining and Arguing* (London: Sage).

Bakhtin, M.M. (1986) *Speech Genres and Other Late Essays* (Austin: University of Texas Press.

Billig, M. (1991) *Ideology and Opinions* (London: Sage).

Billig, M. (1992) *Talking of the Royal Family* (London: Routledge).

Billig, M. (1995) *Banal Nationalism* (London: Sage).

Billig, M. (1996) *Arguing and Thinking* (Cambridge: Cambridge University Press).

Billig, M. (1997a) 'The Dialogic Unconscious: Psycho-analysis, Discursive Psychology and the Nature of Repression', *British Journal of Social Psychology*, vol. 36, pp. 139–159.

Billig, M. (1997b) 'Keeping the White Queen in Play', in Fine, M., Weis, L., Powell, C. and Wong, L.M. (eds) *Off White* (London: Routledge).

Billig, M. (1997c) 'Freud and Dora: Repressing an Oppressed Identity', *Theory, Culture and Society*, vol. 14, pp. 29–55.

Billig, M. (1998) 'Dialogic Repression and the Oedipus Complex: Reinterpreting the Little Hans Case' *Culture and Psychology*, vol. 4, pp. 11–47.

Billig, M. (1999a) *Freudian Repression: Conversation Creating the Unconscious.* (Cambridge: Cambridge University Press).

Billig, M. (1999b) 'Whose Terms? Whose Ordinariness? Rhetoric and Ideology in Conversation Analysis', *Discourse and Society*, vol. 10, pp. 543–558.

Billig, M. (1999c) 'Freud's Response to Reported Incest: The Case of Paul Lorenz, the "Rat Man"', *Psychoanalytic Studies*, vol. 1, no. 2, pp. 145–158.

Billig, M., Condor, S., Edwards, D., Gane, M., Middleton, D. and Radley, A.R. (1988) *Ideological Dilemmas: A Social Psychology of Everyday Thinking* (Sage: London).

Bourdieu, P. (1990) *The Logic of Practice* (Cambridge: Polity Press).

Brown, P. and Levinson, S.C. (1987) *Politeness: Some Universals of Language Usage* (Cambridge: Cambridge University Press).

Decker, H.S. (1991) *Freud, Dora and Vienna 1900* (New York: Free Press).

Dunn, J. (1988) *The Beginnings of Social Understanding* (Oxford: Blackwell).

Eagleton, T. (1991) *Ideology* (London: Verso).

Edwards, D. (1997) *Discourse and Cognition* (London: Sage).

Edwards, D. and Potter, J. (1993) *Discursive Psychology* (London: Sage).

Freud, M. (1957) *Glory Reflected: Sigmund Freud – Man and Father* (London: Angus and Robertson).

Freud, S. (1976) *Jokes and their Relation to the Unconscious* (Harmondsworth: Penguin).

Freud, S. (1990a) 'Analysis of a Phobia in a Five-year-old Boy ("Little Hans")', in *The Penguin Freud Library*, vol. 8, (Harmondsworth: Penguin).

Freud, S. (1990b) 'Fragment of an Analysis of a Case of Hysteria ("Dora")', in *The Penguin Freud Library*, vol. 8 (Harmondsworth: Penguin).

Garfinkel, H. (1967) *Studies in Ethnomethodology* (Englewood Cliffs, NJ: Prentice-Hall).

Gramsci, A. (1971) *Prison Notebooks* (Lawrence and Wishart: London).

Hall, S. (1988) 'The Toad in the Garden: Thatcherism Among the Theorists', in Nelson, C. and Grossberg, L (eds) *Marxism and the Interpretation of Culture* (Basingstoke: Macmillan).

Harré, R. and Gillett, G. (1994) *The Discursive Mind* (London: Sage).

Marx, K. and Engels, F. (1970) *The German Ideology* (London: Lawrence and Wishart).

Middleton, D. and Edwards, D. (1990) 'Conversational Remembering: A Social Psychological Approach', in Middleton D. and Edwards D. (eds) *Collective Remembering* (London: Sage).

Nofsinger, R.E. (1991) *Everyday Conversation* (Newbury Park: Sage).

Parker, I. (1992) *Discourse Dynamics* (London: Routledge).

Perelman, C. and Olbrechts-Tyteca, L. (1971) *The New Rhetoric* (Indiana: University of Notre Dame Press).

Potter, J. (1996) *Representing Reality: Discourse, Rhetoric and Social Constructionism* (London: Sage).

Potter, J. and Edwards, D. (1990) 'Nigel Lawson's Tent: Discourse Analysis, Attribution Theory and the Social Psychology of Fact', *European Journal of Social Psychology*, vol. 20, pp. 405–424.

Potter, J. and Wetherell, M. (1987) *Discourse and Social Psychology* (London: Sage).

Psathas, G. (1995) *Conversation Analysis: The Study of Talk-in-action* (Thousand Oaks: Sage).

Sampson, E.E. (1993) *Celebrating the Other* (London: Sage).

Schiffrin, D. (1984) 'Everyday Argument: The Organisation of Diversity in Talk', in van Dijk, T.A. (ed.) *Handbook of Discourse Analysis* (London: Academic Press).

Shotter, J. (1993a) *The Cultural Politics of Everyday Life* (Milton Keynes: Open University Press).

Shotter, J. (1993b) *Conversational Realities* (London: Sage).

Spence, D.P. (1994) *The Rhetorical Voice of Psychoanalysis* (Cambridge, MA: Harvard University Press).

van Dijk, T.A. (1998) *Ideology* (London: Sage).

Vygotsky, L. (1987) *Thinking and Speech* (New York: Plenum).

Wertsch, J. (1991) *Voices of the Mind* (London: Harvester/Wheatsheaf).

Wilson, J. (1990) *Politically Speaking* (Oxford: Blackwell).

8 The Birth of the Subject and the Use of Truth: Foucault and Social Critique

Mark Haugaard

As was argued in the Introduction, from Marx onwards the concept of ideology has become linked to the existence of a social subject with meaningful autonomy (the humanist problematic) and knowledge which is undistorted by power and domination. The social subject is considered to have internalised knowledge which distorts its perception of reality in a way which is beneficial to a dominant elite – the bourgeoisie in Marxism. It is because the dominated internalise ideology that they willingly participate in the reproduction of structural forms which are contrary to their actual interests. The unmasking of ideology presupposes an active subject who has the capacity to reflect upon the system of knowledge into which they have been socialised and, furthermore, who can replace it with knowledge which does not mirror the distorting effects of domination. Within this perspective, social critique is practised by using truth to unmask the distorting effects of domination. Philosophically speaking, truth is a view from 'nowhere'. If something is true, it is true irrespective of particular 'local' culturally constituted knowledges and, as a consequence, cannot mirror deformation brought about by power and domination.

Social critique also presupposes a subject who has the capacity to transcend local context. If, as postmodernists argue, the social subject is the mere effect of the systems of thought into which they are socialised, they cannot distance themselves from previously internalised knowledge. They become like flotsam and jetsam upon a sea of meaning which tosses them from one horizon to the next. In contrast to this, the more autonomous subject of ideology is an agent who has the capacity to transcend local contextuality and critically evaluate it. As I have argued elsewhere (Haugaard, 1997), this subject need not transcend local meaning entirely but, rather, should be considered more as a person on a raft who has the capacity to rebuild, and consequently transform, their craft without ever getting off it. It is a question of mirroring meanings and contexts against each other in a manner which makes agents self-conscious of the way in which specific meanings are implicated in relations of domination. 'Local' truths become revealed as covert 'wills to power' in a process which entails mirroring 'truths' and systems of thought against each other. This consciousness raising is not some obscure process but, rather, reflects aspects of everyday life. As has been argued by Giddens (1984), social consciousness comprises both a tacit aspect (practical consciousness) and knowledge which we can put into words (discursive consciousness). These are not hermetically sealed aspects of social knowledge but, rather, are characterised by a continual flow of information from one to the other. When we learn a foreign language, or visit an unfamiliar culture, we use discursive consciousness knowledge for practical consciousness tasks. Similarly, but in reverse, when we read Goffman's descriptions of everyday life or Foucault's description of the Panopticon, our tacit knowledge of social life is rendered discursive – it is a process of recognition of what 'we already know'. This consciousness raising, or move from practical consciousness to discursive consciousness, has a radical aspect and undermines relations of domination because the routine reproduction of meaning and structure suddenly becomes subject to critical scrutiny. The things which individuals have always done because 'that's the way we do things around here' are suddenly problematised.

However, this process presupposes an agent who has the capacity to evaluate relative truth claims. If Foucault's description of the Panopticon is to have radical implications, the reader must believe that this is not some 'arbitrary' new description. However, this need not necessitate absolute truth but, rather, the ability to balance interpretative horizons against each other. As was argued by Weber, actors switch rationalities all the time. They are not made up of one continuous interpretative horizon – they may be driven by instrumental rationality during the day and affective action in the evening. Following Bauman (1989) and Habermas (1984, 1987), systematic failure to switch interpretative horizon is what makes it possible for actors to collaborate in the reproduction of systems of domination which they never evaluate – the 'ordinary German' during the Holocaust and the disenchanted being who allows 'system rationality' to colonise the 'life world'. In contrast, social critics can stand on one part of their interpretative raft while they 'saw up' another part for the sake of a better (more truthful and egalitarian) vision of how their raft should be constructed (Haugaard, 1997, pp. 163–187).

When we read Foucault's histories they have the effect on the reader of social critique. However, Foucault's theoretical insistence, that there is no truth without power and the 'death of the subject', would appear to preclude such a possibility. It has frequently been argued that Foucault's relativisation of truth undermines the episte-mological foundations of his critique of modern knowledge. As has been observed by Taylor, the '... regime-relativity of truth means that we cannot raise the banner of truth against our own regime' (Taylor, 1984, p. 176). It is also a criticism frequently levelled at Foucault's work that the death of the subject undermines the possibility of the type of radical political action which, on another level, Foucault advocates – this lies at the core of the conservative implications of Foucault's work noted by Habermas and Nancy Fraser (Kelly, 1994).

In this chapter we shall examine Foucault's concept of 'truth' and his declared death of the subject from a different perspective than characterises this form of critique. We shall take it as given that the total relativisation of truth entails an undermining of the epistemo-logical foundations of radical critique and accept that there is an inevitable conservatism inherent in the hypothesis of the death of the subject. We shall look at the broader issue of whether the type of social critique to which Foucault was committed actually entails either the death of the subject or deep philosophical relativism. In a certain sense, this can be regarded as a defence of Foucault against postmodern trends in his work which undermine its utility for the project of critical theory and critique of ideology. While it is beyond dispute that Foucault perceived himself as a radical philosophical relativist and that he was strongly committed to the idea of the death of the subject, we shall argue that neither are actually intrinsic to the logic of the theoretical position which Foucault develops in his genealogical histories. The point of this argument is not primarily to defend or criticise Foucault: the issue is much wider than the work of a particular author. If we recognise, as Foucault did, that relations of domination are recreated through the reproduction of systems of meaning and reinforced through the language of truth production, we need to know if this recognition is necessarily self-defeating. While Foucault presented his analysis in terms that have self-defeating implications, we shall argue that these self-defeating implications are not inherent to such a perception of relations of domination and, furthermore, that the actual content of Foucault's genealogy offers evidence to support such a thesis. We shall argue that the genealogical method represents a birth of the subject in the sense that the subject has autonomy not only to act creatively as a *re*producer of meaning but, more significantly, also as a *creator* of new meaning. With regard to truth, Foucault's work tells us nothing concerning the philosophical issues which lead to relativism. This is theoretically important because, once this is realised, Foucault's work can be used as a source of critique by those who hold neither with the death of the subject nor with deep philosophical relativism.[1]

Foucault's archaeological work is a form of radical critique where our taken-for-granted reality – the systems of knowledge which shape tacit perceptions of the world – are thrown open to question. This is done by showing us '... how that-which-is has not always been i.e., that the things which seem most evident to us are always formed in the confluence of encounters ...' and that these perceptions have been made and, as a consequence, they can also be unmade (Foucault, 1988, pp. 36–37). It is a form of critique which he describes as the 'flushing out' of thought whereby he shows us that what we take for granted as self-evident is in fact not so (Foucault, 1988, p.155).

If we consider the social agent's interpretative horizon as constituted through frameworks of meaning, a Foucauldian social critique is a form of interrogation of that horizon. What Foucault called the historical a priori (Foucault, 1970, pp. xv–xxiv) are the tacit meanings which make us see the world the way we do. The historical a priori is our taken-for-granted reality which constitutes us as we are.

One of Foucault's techniques for making us question our historical a priori is to give his readers a jolt by thrusting them into an alternative reality. For instance, *The Order of Things* begins with a bizarre and puzzling quotation from Borges about

> ... a 'certain Chinese encyclopaedia' in which it is written that 'animals are divided into: (a) belonging to the emperor, (b) embalmed, (c) tame, (d) suckling pigs, (e) sirens, (f) fabulous, (g) stray dogs, (h) included in the present classification, (i) frenzied, (j) innumerable, (k) drawn with a very fine camel hair brush, (l) *et cetera*, (m) having just broken the water pitcher, (n) that from a long way off look like flies.' (Foucault, 1970, p. xv)

For us the passage is impossible to comprehend because the ordering device which could link, for instance, 'stray dogs' with 'having just broken the water pitcher', is entirely absent. We do not know what it means to see the world in this way. We cannot comprehend because, to use Heideggerian language, the being-in-the-world of the Chinese encyclopaedist is entirely different from our being-in-the-world. Because the former's being-in-the-world is so entirely different from our own, we are confronted with the stark fact that it is possible to see reality, and to be, in an entirely different way from the way we see and are. The consequence of such a confrontation with radical difference of being is to make 'that-which-is appear as something which might not be or that might not be as it is' (Foucault, 1988, p. 37) and, in so doing, we realise that our taken-for-granted reality is a historical construct which has been made and, as a consequence can be unmade. Our way of perceiving the world and our method of reason '... reside on a base of human practice and history; and that since these things have been made, they can be unmade, as long as we know how it is that they were made' (p. 37).

Foucault's method of social critique is radical in the sense that he performs a critique of the interpretative framework which constitutes our horizon of meaning and being. It is not only what we say which is interrogated, but the system of meaning which we use to say what we do which is subject to critique. However, this form of social critique is theoretically deeply problematic because it raises the problem of meaning and social stability: if Foucauldian critique is to have a political purpose then we must presuppose that it is possible to change these meanings.

Meaning, of course, is not intrinsic to the world. The constitution of meaning is contingent across space (in different geographically situated cultures) and time (the historical evolution of thought which Foucault documents). However, if meaning is arbitrary and contingent, as is evidenced by differences of meaning, we are confronted with the problem of the stability of meaning. This is *the* problem of social theory – the problem of social order – whereby we have to account for the fact that meaning does not disintegrate even though it is both conventional and historically contingent. This is made particularly problematic if we take seriously the Foucauldian point that meanings entail relations of domination and subjectification. It seems almost logical to suppose that dominated social actors might simply choose to opt out of social order. When confronted with meanings which disadvantage them, one could almost imagine disadvantaged social actors saying words to the effect, 'Sorry, that's all arbitrary and contingent social convention, I don't accept it!' The aggregate consequence would be praxiological chaos, which clearly does not happen – social order is reproduced with remarkable (though, significantly, not total) regularity. Obviously coercion can, to an extent, explain why actors do not 'opt out' of social order but it does not do so in its entirety – social order is not simply recreated through the coercion of the losers by the winners.

In Foucault's archaeology the answer to the problem of social order is a holistic systemic solution: social order is reproduced as a consequence of its systemic properties. Because meanings are constituted relationally it is not possible for individual actors to contest specific meanings. Social change only happens systemically as one system replaces another – what Foucault termed discontinuity. Alternatively, we have stability.

If we follow Wittgenstein's private language argument to its logical conclusion, it is impossible to give meaning to a word by confronting it with an external nonlinguistic context. Hence, new meanings are never introduced externally, with the consequence that languages are self-reproducing local ways of life.[2] Similarly, in Sausurre the meaning of a word is created by its membership of a linguistic system in which the meaning of each word is constituted through relational difference from other words within the system:

> ... in language there are only differences. Even more important: a difference generally implies positive terms between which the difference is set up; but in language there are only differences without positive terms. Whether we take the signifier or the signified, language has neither ideas nor sounds that existed before the linguistic system, but only conceptual or phonic differences that have issued from the system. (Saussure, 1964, p. 120)

Consequently, truly new meaning is an impossibility: we are simply recyclers of already preconstituted meanings. Meaning is not created by the intention of the speaker and, while it has to be accepted that the social subject is the *re*producer of meaning, she is never the creator of meaning.[3]

This systemic view is prominent in Foucault's archaeology. Here the greater system, which confers meaning through relational difference, is the *episteme*, and the base subunits (the theoretical equivalent of words in Saussure) are statements. In a manner theoretically similar to words in language, statements confer meaning upon each other:

There is no statement in general, no free, neutral, independent statement; but a statement always belongs to a series or a whole, always plays a role among other statements, deriving support from them and distinguishing itself from them: it is always part of a network of statements, in which it has a role, however minimal it may be, to play. (Foucault, 1989, p. 99)

In a manner which is analogous to Sausurre's' analysis of language, in the archaeological *episteme* all statements refer to each other and preclude the truly creative act of making a statement which is non-epistemic. The social subject is trapped inside her particular epistemic context and is, in this sense, dead. This explains how, despite their conventional and contingent nature, systems of meaning remain stable. However, it does so much too effectively in the sense that it is a theoretisation of systemic stability which entails that individuals are epistemically trapped and, hence, the enterprise of radical critique is an impossibility. However, I would now suggest that the genealogy contains an implicit way out of this problem.

In the genealogy, social change is linked to power and truth. Power is not viewed as a teleological source of social change. Power has no essence and is not situated anywhere and, hence, there is no teleology of power (Foucault, 1981, p. 92). Power has to do with struggle (Foucault, 1979, pp. 26–27) and *is always exercised* (Foucault, 1980, p. 89). According to this perception, power is '... the reign of peace in civil society ...' whereby power is the reinscription of the rules of war. In other words, power is war by other means (Foucault, 1980, p. 90).

In the genealogy there are two levels of conflict. There are the conflicts which take place within a regime of truth production and there is the deeper conflict at the level of meaning. At the latter level '... power produces: it produces reality: it produces domains of objects and rituals of truth' (Foucault, 1979, p. 194). This distinction between deep conflict and more superficial conflict can be illustrated by analogy with chess. In chess, actors prevail over one another within certain rules and local frameworks of meaning. There is no deeper conflict in the sense that meaning and rules are not thrown open to question but, rather, they facilitate conflict between the players. In the game of chess we can become better and better players and, in this way, increase our local power. However, unlike in social life, it is not possible to engage in conflict over meaning. The latter is a conflict which is frequently motivated by the desire to create new relations of domination by making it possible to win in new ways. It is with reference to distinction between these levels of conflict that we should interpret Foucault's observation that the conflict between Marx and the bourgeois economists was a storm in a children's paddling pool (Foucault, 1970, p. 262). That particular conflict presupposed the reproduction of a shared framework of meaning. It was like a game of chess where there was great skill but no questioning of the system of meaning which defined the parameters of the conflict.

Integral to power as the production of reality, or interpretative frameworks, is the role of truth – politics and power are a struggle for truth. '"Truth" is to be understood as a system of ordered procedures for the production, regulation, distribution and operation of statements' (Foucault, 1980, p. 133). The struggle for domination, which constitutes the essence of power, is a struggle for truth. 'Truth' is linked in a circular relation with systems of power which produce and sustain it, and to the effects of power which induce and which extend it: a 'régime' of truth (p. 133).

This perceived link between power and truth provides a potential way out of total systemic determinism. Conceptual space is created for social action of the type which entails a change of meaning. The battle for truth can be used to encode the constitution of meaning because of the nonrelative status which historically has always been accorded to truth. If the creation of new meaning is linked to truth, it is not systemically derived but, in its place, an illusion is created that meaning is somehow intrinsic to the newly created object of knowledge. If the case can be made that a new meaning is not merely a proposed new convention, then there is compelling reason for others to accept it. As a consequence of its status as a 'view from nowhere' (as an extra-systemic source of meaning) truth becomes the foundation for the introduction of new meaning into conventional systems of meaning.

Truth is not, of course, some external teleological source as, for instance, reason is for Hegel. Rather, it exists at the level of local strategies. Actors struggle to create new objects of meaning because the existence of particular objects as carriers of meaning in some way benefits them. In this context we can make use of Bourdieu's extended use of the word 'capital'.[4] If we take capital as referring to a local resource which a select number of actors have exclusive use of, the struggle over production of meaning is part of a system-wide struggle over capital. Individual actors create new objects in order to tap into new sources of capital. To see how this takes place let us take the instance of Pierre Rivière, who was accused and convicted of murdering his mother and two sisters (Foucault, 1975). What interested Foucault concerning the Rivière case was the way in which experts insisted on producing a large body of documents concerning the life of Rivière. It is significant that these documents were not necessary for the conviction – the guilt of Rivière was beyond dispute and it was quite evident that the judge in the case did not know what to do with these documents. The importance of this body of knowledge constructed around the person of Rivière lay in its contribution to the creation of a new system of meaning (criminology) which contained a new field of objects from which truth could be obtained – the delinquent, the perpetual offender and the dangerous individual. In other words, Pierre Rivière was a new object or carrier of meaning which a certain group of individuals (would-be criminologists, psychologists and sociologists) fought to create for the purpose of producing a new source of capital. The disciplines of criminology, psychology and sociology became resources which gave specific actors (criminologists, psychologists and sociologists) capital in the form of a monopoly on expertise.

In the modern period, objects of meaning include living beings who configure the interpretative horizon of the newly created 'sciences of man'. For the specialists in the 'science of man' the fight for creation of these objects is motivated by a desire for capital, while the unintended effect of this fight for capital is the subjectification of the living beings as they become objects of truth.

Meaning and methods of truth production circumscribe possibilities of conflict. They tame conflict by preventing it from degenerating into war. In this case, war is the equivalent of praxiological chaos or the total degeneration of social order. Truth creates new objects around which a new order can be created without praxiological degeneration by providing a definite threshold for systemic change. Actors cannot simply create new objects of meaning as alternative conventional ways of life – this would lead to praxiological chaos. Truth provides a brake upon systemic change. We either have systemic stability whereby meanings are simply reproduced or, in exceptional circumstances, new meaning is created through the discovery of new objects of truth. These additions to, or changes of, the social system happen as the consequence of local conflicts which are carried out by individual actors fighting to manufacture capital through the creation of a new social order which is presented as something other than an arbitrary set of conventions through a link to truth.

It is because Foucault is interested in deep conflicts – conflicts over meaning – that his histories are populated with names which are unfamiliar to us. Conventional histories of ideas document local victories of great players, but what they leave out are the names of those whose local conflicts contribute to the creation of new meanings and which, in turn, constitute the context of the victories and defeats within shared systems of meaning and truth production. The big names of conventional history are like chess champions who play brilliantly within the rules of the game but are not responsible for the creation of the system of meaning which they reproduce.

Pierre Rivière is an instance of what Foucault termed the 'dangerous individual'.[5] As an object, the dangerous individual lives among us as a threat which we need experts to identify and manage. For the would-be experts this object of knowledge entails the creation of a body of expertise which constitutes capital. It is not possible to set oneself up as an expert upon any object. It has to be proved that this object represents something other than a personal whim, and this is achieved by the link to truth.[6] As a 'view from nowhere' or, more specifically, as a view from outside the system of convention, the 'dangerous individual' does not represent the mere subjectivity of those for whom it constitutes a source of capital.

The struggle for new meaning through truth production provides a method whereby social change can take place without presupposing the disintegration of social order. The individual does not simply introduce new arbitrary objects as carriers of meaning within social order but does so by linking these new objects to a stable point outside existing social order. This is done without any presupposed grand teleological project of historical change: actors engage in this struggle over the processes of truth production because they have vested interests in creating new objects of knowledge which they can use as sources of capital. Interpreted in this way, the social subject is not decentred from, or irrelevant to, the creation of meaning but the creator of new meaning through participation in local struggles for new sources of capital.

The names which Foucault writes into history are active social subjects, not the decentred subjects presupposed by the death of the subject. However, it may be thought that this birth of the subject appears to offer little hope for the creation of a better society. While we have shown that the proposition of an active social subject does not entail the conservatism deriving from determinism (Habermas' and Fraser's point), this may appear to be a struggle which is going nowhere because the link between power and truth entails a nihilistic relativisation of truth (Taylor's objection). However, contrary to appearances (and to Foucault's own perceptions), this is not theoretically the case.

In the genealogy, the use of truth is analysed. Genealogical histories are an account of how truth is deployed in the struggle over meaning. As Foucault observes: following Nietzsche, he does not concern himself with 'What is the surest path to truth?' but rather, 'What is the hazardous career that Truth has followed?' (Foucault, 1980, p. 66; 1988, p. 107). However, I would argue that answering the question 'What is the surest path to truth?' involves a very different discourse (to use Foucault's term) or language game (to use Wittgensteinian terminology) than is entailed by the question 'What is the hazardous career that Truth has followed?' In order to make this distinction clearer, let us term the former a 'philosophical' discourse or language game and the latter a 'sociological' one: the philosopher is interested in the surest path to truth, whereas the sociologist is preoccupied with the *use which people make of truth* or, in the case of historical sociology, *the use which actors have made of truth*.

In the philosophical-discourse formation the question of truth is one concerning epistemology, whereas in the sociological-discourse formation the investigation is ultimately an *empirical* one concerning behaviour, even if the latter is theoretically grounded. Foucault documents conflicts, strategies of domination and power relations which are inextricably bound up with regimes of truth production – he analyses the process of truth production within the discourse formation of historical sociology. However, the local truths of historical sociology do not tell us anything concerning the philosophical status of truth. As Foucault was at great pains to observe, a statement made in one discursive formation has an entirely different meaning from the same statement made in a different discursive formation. The statement that 'truth is a disguised will to power' or that 'truth is inextricably bound up with relations of domination' has an entirely different meaning within the discourse of historical sociology than it does in philosophy. *It is only in the latter that such statements entail relativism.* By following the hazardous career of truth, Foucault does not give us any information on the surest way to truth nor does he commit us to the conclusion that there is no such path.

While it is a valid observation that the philosophical analysis of truth has the potential to impact upon the sociological discourse concerning truth, the reverse is not the case. Answering sociological questions concerning truth tells us nothing about its epistemological status. To take some parallels: Durkheim held that a shared concept of truth reinforced social integration, without being a philosophical relativist; Weber argued that certain forms of rationality reinforce relations of domination, without embracing philosophical irrationalism (of the romantic, or any other, variety) and, similarly, anthropologists may hold that a belief in God reinforces social solidarity, without committing themselves to atheism.

This distinction between sociology and philosophy entails that it is possible both to observe *sociologically* that truth is used to initiate social change and, simultaneously, to maintain that there is such a thing as philosophical truth. Once this distinction is realised it is not contradictory to argue that a social critique which documents the link between truth and power is in itself true. Obviously the sociological analysis should make us suspicious of truth (which is the only proper mindset of a critical theorist) but will not lead us to reject the possibility of it. Furthermore, the knowledge that power and truth are invariably linked has the positive aspect that the successful fight for truth by a radical critical theory will, if it can establish its objects of truth, change relations of domination.

In conclusion, the struggle which Foucault describes in his genealogy entails active social actors, the existence of whom is inconsistent with the death of the subject; and his analysis of truth is entirely neutral on the philosophical questions which have the potential to lead to relativism. This implies that the type of social critique which Foucault's genealogical histories represent is not necessarily self-defeating. It is theoretically possible to engage in Foucauldian historical social critique and, simultaneously, to maintain that what is said is true. Furthermore, the concept of social agency implicit in this form of critique does not foreclose the possibility of radical political action. In short, Foucault's histories can be used as important sources of critique by those who are neither theoretically committed to postmodern philosophical relativism nor to the death of the subject. Foucault's genealogical observations are commensurable with the broad tradition of modern critical theory which presupposes ideology and, as a consequence, has among its premises an active social subject and a commitment to philosophical truth, even if this was not evident to Foucault. The death of the subject and the philosophical relativisation of truth are shadows of the dead living on in the incompatible theoretical logic of Foucault's genealogical histories.

NOTES

1. Some of the ideas used in this chapter are developed at greater length, but in a different context, in Haugaard (1997).
2. In his *Contingency, Irony and Solidarity* (1989, p. 41) Rorty argues that Wittgenstein's private language argument precludes the possibility of the type of 'true' originality which entails changes of meaning.
3. Not only did Saussure argue that new meaning is entirely beyond the scope of individual speakers but he even argued that it is outside the scope of a community of speakers: 'No individual, even if he willed it, could modify in any way at all the choice [of words] that has been made: and what is more, the community itself cannot so much as change a single word; it is bound to existing language' (Saussure, 1964, p. 71).
4. Bourdieu (1986) argues that there are three forms of capital. We will not follow in this, as I see no intrinsic reason for the hypothesis that there are three, as opposed to any other number, of types of capital.
5. For other instances of the discovery of the dangerous individual in the early part of the nineteenth century, see Foucault (1988, pp. 128–129).
6. It is not only the dangerous individual who is created at the time of the birth of the 'sciences of man'. For instance, in the field of sexuality, the Lapcourt case performs a theoretically parallel function to the Rivière case. See Foucault (1981, pp. 31–32).

REFERENCES

Bauman, Z. (1989) *Modernity and the Holocaust* (Cambridge: Polity).

Bourdieu, P. (1986) 'The Forms of Capital' in Richardson, J.G. (ed.) *Handbook of Theory and Research for the Sociology of Education* (New York: Greenwood).

Foucault, M. (1970) *The Order of Things* (London: Routledge).

Foucault, M. (ed.) (1975) *I, Pierre Rivière, Having Slaughtered my Mother, my Sister and my Brother … A Case of Parricide in the 19th Century* (Harmondsworth: Penguin).

Foucault, M. (1979) *Discipline and Punish: The Birth of the Prison* (Harmondsworth: Penguin).

Foucault, M. (1980) *Power/Knowledge: Selected Interviews and Other Writings 1972–1977*, in Gordon, C. (ed.) (Brighton: Harvester Press).

Foucault, M. (1981) *The History of Sexuality Volume 1: An Introduction* (Harmondsworth: Penguin).

Foucault, M. (1988) *Michel Foucault: Politics, Philosophy, Culture* (ed. L.D. Kritzman) (London: Routledge).

Giddens, A. (1984) *The Constitution of Society* (Cambridge: Polity).

Habermas, J. (1984) *The Theory of Communicative Action: Vol. I, Reason and the Rationalization of Society* (Cambridge: Polity).

Habermas, J. (1987) *The Theory of Communicative Action: Vol. II, The Critique of Functionalist Reason* (Cambridge: Polity).

Haugaard, M. (1997) *The Constitution of Power* (Manchester: Manchester University Press).

Kelly, M. (1994) *Critique and Power: Recasting the Foucault/Habermas Debate* (Cambridge Mass.: MIT Press).

Rorty, R. (1989) *Contingency, Irony and Solidarity* (Cambridge: Cambridge University Press).

Saussure, F. de (1964) *Course in General Linguistics* (London: Peter Owen Limited).

Taylor, C. (1984) 'Foucault on Freedom and Truth', *Political Theory*, vol. 12, no. 2, pp. 152–183.

Notes on Contributors

Michael Billig is Professor at the Department of Social Sciences, Loughborough University. He is author and editor of numerous books including *Ideology and Opinions* (Sage, 1991), *Arguing and Thinking* (CUP, 1996), *Banal Nationalism* (Sage, 1997), *Freudian Repression* (CUP, 1999) and *Rock'n'Roll Jews* (Five Leaves, 2000).

Diana Coole is Professor of Political Theory at Queen Mary and Westfield College, University of London. Her most recent work is *Negativity and Politics: Dionysus and Dialectics from Kant to Poststructuralism* (Routledge, 2000). She is currently writing a book on Merleau-Ponty and the Political.

Mark Haugaard is a Lecturer in the Department of Political Science and Sociology, National University of Ireland, Galway. He is author of *The Constitution of Power* (Manchester University Press, 1997) and *Structures, Restructuration and Social Power* (Aldershot, 1992), and co-editor of *Power in Contemporary Politics* (Sage, 2000).

Kieran Keohane is a Statutory Lecturer in the Department of Sociology, National University of Ireland, Cork. He is author of *Symptoms of Canada* (Toronto University Press, 1997) and of many articles on social and political theory.

Iain MacKenzie is a Lecturer in Politics at Queen's University, Belfast. He is author of articles on Deleuze and Guattari and co-author of *Contemporary Social and Political Theory: An Introduction* (Open University Press, 1999).

Sinisa Malešević is a Lecturer in the Department of Political Science and Sociology, National University of Ireland, Galway. He is author of *Ideology, Legitimacy and the New State* (Frank Cass, 2002) and of articles on ethnicity, nationalism and sociological theory. He is also editor of *Culture in Central and Eastern Europe: Institutional and Value Changes* (IMO, 1997).

Robert Porter is a Lecturer in Communications at University of Ulster. His work is on the social and political consequences of Deleuze and Guattari's constructivist philosophy.

Caroline Williams is a Lecturer in Political Theory at Queen Mary and Westfield College, University of London. She is author of *Contemporary French Philosophy: Modernity and the Persistence of the Subject* (Athlone Press, 2001) and has published essays on Lacanian psychoanalysis, selfhood and subjectivity.

Index

Compiled by Auriol Griffith-Jones